Rioting in North-East Wales
1536-1918

Rioting in North-East Wales, 1536-1918

Tim Jones

WREXHAM

First published in Wales in 1997
by
BRIDGE BOOKS
61 Park Avenue
Wrexham
LL12 7AW

ISBN 1-872424-55-4

A CIP catalogue entry for this book
is available from the British Library

Printed and bound by
MFP, Stretford, Manchester

CONTENTS

ACKNOWLEDGEMENTS

My thanks for their valuable assistance to the staffs of the Flintshire Record Office, Hawarden and the Denbighshire Record Office, Ruthin; the Flintshire, Denbighshire and Wrexham County Libraries; the National Library of Wales, Aberystwyth; and in particular to Mr C J Williams, Mr K Matthias, Mr D Castledine, Ms E Pettitt, Mr P Mason, Ms F Wilkinson-Buckley, Mr N Walker and Mr W Alister Williams.

My greatest thanks as ever go to my family for their moral and financial support, especially Mr & Mrs R L Jones, Mr W A Jones and Mr & Mrs R R Fisher.

Finally, all illustrative material is reproduced from the private local history collection of Mr W A Jones, the Denbighshire Record Office and the W Alister Williams Collection.

Timothy Llewellyn Jones, 1997.

Chronology of known Riots and Ructions in north-east Wales, 1536-1918

IRO (In the reign of) Henry VIII, (1509-47) Halchdyn: Llanrhaidr-yn-Cinmeirche

1537	Denbigh
c1533/8	Holt

IRO Philip & Mary, (1553-58)   Hanmer

IRO Elizabeth I, (1558-1603)   Chirk: Denbigh: Holywell: Llandegla: Wrexham

1544	St George (Llansansior)
1546	Cefn Du
1547	Segrwyd
1550	Esclusham
1558	Llansilin
1575	Gresford
1578	Chirk, Nantglyn
1580	Flint
1584	Sgrwgan
1589	Holywell: Valle Crucis
1590	Esclusham: Llansilin: Ruabon: Ruthin: Sycharth: Wrexham
1591	Denbigh: Hafodywern (Wrexham)
1592	Llansilin
1593	Cilcen: Denbigh: Maes-y-gwig: Llandegla: Trovarth
1594	Abergele: Burton: Cymmo: Glyndyfrdwy: Glynfechan: Gwytherin: Llanarmon Dyffryn Ceiriog: Llanarmon Dyffryn Ceiriog: Llanelidan: Llangollen: Llansantffraid Glyndyfrdwy: Ruabon: Sgrwgan: Sgrwgan: Valle Crucis
1595	Denbigh: Llanelidan: Llanelidan: Morton:Sgrwgan
1596	Sutton
1597	Llanbedr Dyffryn Clwyd
1598	Ruthin: Ysceifiog
1599	Denbigh: Denbigh: Ruabon
1600	Cefn-mawr: Denbigh: Ruthin
1601	Wrexham
1602	Denbigh: Denbigh: Llansannan

IRO James I, (1603-25)   Aberwheeler: Bettisfield: Bodfari: Bodrhyddan: Caerwys: Ffrith(?): Hanmer: Henllan: Henllan: Hope: Llanasa: Llanasa: Llansilin: Llewerllyd: Llewerllyd: Rhuddlan: Ruthin: Wrexham: Ysceifiog(?)

1629	Ewloe

1691	Denbigh
1690s	Wrexham
1702	Wrexham
1705	Wrexham
1709	Erddig: Wrexham
1710	Wrexham
1711	Galltegfa
1715	Ruabon: Wrexham: Wrexham
1716	Wrexham: Wrexham
1720	Wrexham
1721	Llannefydd
1722	Wrexham
1724	Granllyn
1734	Caergwrle: Flint: Mold
1737	Flint
1740	Abergele: Cwm: Denbigh: Dyserth: Henllan: Holywell: Llannefydd: Mostyn: Prestatyn: Rhuddlan: Rhyl: St Asaph: Trelawnyd: Wrexham: Wrexham
1745	Hawarden
c1750	Denbigh
1753	Threapwood
1767	Hawarden
1776	Wrexham
1778	Flint
1789	Denbigh: East Denbighshire: East Flintshire: Holywell: Wrexham
c1790	Wrexham
1793	Caergwrle: Flint: Hope: Mold: Penyffordd: Pontblyddyn
1795	Abergele: Denbigh: Mold: Rhuddlan: Wrexham
1796	Hawarden: Mold: Rhuddlan
1801	Bagillt: Denbigh: Holywell: Rhosymedre: Towyn
1802	Buckley
1809	Henllan
1814	St George (Llansansior)
1815	Denbigh
1816	Northop: Wrexham
1817	Brymbo: Wrexham
1819	Bagillt: Holywell
1822	Brymbo: Halkyn: Holywell
1825	Mold
1825-26	Hawarden: Holywell: Mold
1826	Coed Talon: Denbigh: Mold
1826-27	Halkyn: Leeswood
1828	Flintshire
1830	Acrefair: Brymbo: Flintshire: Leeswood: Mold: Rhos: Ruabon
1831	Acrefair: Brymbo: Brymbo: Cefn-mawr: Chirk: Holywell: Mold: Mold: Mold: Mostyn: Newbridge: Overton Bridge: Rhos: Wrexham
1832	Rhos
1839	Denbigh: Wrexham
1840	Chirk: Mold: Ruabon
1842	Hawarden
1843	Denbighshire: Flintshire: Maerdy

1844	Greenfield: Hawarden: Holywell: Meliden: Mold: Northop
1850	Brymbo: Holywell
1851	Treuddyn
1852	Holywell: Meliden
1852-54	Denbigh
1856	Acrefair: Dyserth: Talargoch: Tywyn
1859	Ruabon
1863	Coed Talon: Leeswood: Mold
1863-65	Denbighshire: Flintshire
1864	Mostyn
1866	Halkyn
1867	Halkyn
1868	Ruabon: Wrexham
1869	Leeswood: Mold
1875	Brymbo
1878	Rhos
1882	Coedpoeth: Moss: Ruabon
1884-85	Buckley
1885	Brymbo: Brymbo
1886	Abergele: Brymbo: Colwyn Bay: Llanarmon-yn-Iâl: Llanarmon-yn-Iâl: Llandrillo-yn-Rhos: Llanfair Dyffryn Clwyd: Mostyn: Mostyn: Whitford
1887	Bodfari: ?Caergwrle: Corwen: Denbigh: Gwernaffield: Holywell: Llandrillo: Llangwm: Mochdre: Rhyl: St Asaph: Tremeirchion
1888	Caerwys: Denbigh: Holywell: Llanferres: Llangwm: Llannefydd: Llansannan: Ruthin
1889	Llanferres: Llanfihangel Glyn Myfyr
1890	Derwen: Llanferres: Llannefydd: Llannefydd: Llannefydd
1891	Llannefydd
1893	Brymbo: Leeswood: Wrexham
1894	Buckley
1910	Hawarden: Hawarden
1911	Hawarden
1912	Chirk
1915	Rhyl

Introduction: The nature of the traditional riot

People have gathered in groups and caused violent and tumultuous disorder, or rioted, throughout history. They have done so for a whole host of political, economic, social, psychological and other reasons, and Wales has been no exception. The most celebrated Welsh riots in the years between the Act of Union in 1536 and the end of the First World War in 1918 occurred in south Wales, and included the Merthyr and Newport Risings of 1831 and 1839 and the Chartist and Rebecca Riots of the 1830s and 1840s. But while these episodes were significant for their sometimes lethal violence and their lasting national political and psychological impacts, the 'rabbles' of north-east Wales also participated in more than their fair share of riots and ructions between 1536 and 1918,[1] which should not be eclipsed by the spectacular and more famous disturbances of south Wales. Indeed, while rioting in England and Wales 'rarely (resulted in) ... taking (of) lives' in the period between the first Jacobite Rebellion of 1715 and the emergence of widespread, coordinated industrial disputes from about 1830, a number of the riots in the old counties[2] of Denbighshire,[3] Flintshire,[4] and a small part of old Merionethshire,[5] were bloody affairs and involved a number of fatalities.

Few of the riots that broke out in Britain before the 19th century were manifestations of rebellion or posed a direct threat to the position of the political Establishment. But although rioting did not lead to the overthrow of the 'upper orders' as it did across the Channel in 1789, outbreaks of popular violence motivated by objectives other than revolt did cause the ruling classes grave anxiety and fear, especially when they perceived themselves to be the target of civil dissension. Indeed, before the Victorian era the mob more often than not achieved their socio-economic or other limited aims by means of their violent outbursts, and very few of the rioters were ever brought to book. The inadequacies of the legal system and the fact that the 'lower orders' had 'no political rights ... no(r) other means of redress of grievance' meant that riots were regarded as, if not 'normal', certainly an accepted and familiar method of protest, and an expression of their right to acquire 'natural justice'. Cottagers, small hold farmers, colliers, craftsmen, the poor, and others, often came together to riot if a community or some of its members felt that an aspect of their lives was being threatened or harmed. They either acted spontaneously or gathered through word of mouth at local meeting places like markets, pubs or shops, where they were organised by leaders who became 'heroes of the crowd'. Such men roused them and gave them direction through speeches, and they allotted targets for attack, such as landowners' farm buildings or other assets and, especially from the late 18th century onwards, industrialists' houses or premises, which were burned, demolished or ransacked.[6]

Early riots in north-east Wales

The available documentary evidence covering the earlier part of this study is unsurprisingly less complete than that for later years, and so there are fewer details about the many riots that occurred then. And, although the extensive volumes of legal proceedings that were produced by various contemporary judicial organs may contain references to rioting, as G M Griffiths has pointed out, while 'a lengthy catalogue of minor and major crimes committed in the county could be produced', as yet no complete index of cases of rioting in the records of numerous public archives has been written, and like Griffiths 'this I do not intend to do'. Nonetheless, for the purposes of this survey it is sufficient that all known recorded riots in north-east Wales are included.[7]

Cases dealing with riot and other major public disorders rarely went before the Court of Quarter Sessions, which dealt on the whole with 'petty' crimes, (although these could include crimes of violence).[8] Instead, instances of 'riot and affray' were usually heard by a variety of higher legal institutions after 1535. Under the terms of the Acts of Union between England and Wales the Welsh were assigned the same 'freedoms, liberties, rights and privileges and laws' as the English, and henceforth 'they were not required to go to London to have their (more serious) cases tried. Wales was divided into four Circuits, with judges who came to each at regular intervals and administered a common justice to all. The Court of Great Sessions convened twice every year in north-east Wales, initially covering north-eastern Denbighshire, all of Flintshire and Merionethshire, and later Chester as well, and its judges operated in this capacity until 1830.[9] In addition, there were other bodies that administered the law until the Great Civil War, the most important for this study being the Star Chamber of the Privy Council, and the Council in the Marches of Wales. The 'Star Chamber was a central prerogative court (or ultimate court of appeal) acting as the judicial section of the Privy Council. Its main purpose ... (was) to bring some show of justice into the process of the development of Wales under the Tudor policy of Union and local self-government', although it only really got into its stride as a popular 'court of appeal from local and central courts' from the middle years of the reign of Elizabeth I onwards.[10] The Star Chamber 'did not wholly succeed in curbing the rapacity of the tudor gentry', who often displayed 'a strain of barbarism' and appear to have played quite a significant role in numerous riotous endeavours in the region. Another body called the Council in the Marches was designed specifically to hear cases of alleged affray, assault, riot, rout (or disorderly crowds), forcible entry onto property and other major violent crimes. In fulfilling this role the Council was meant to try to keep the more ebullient elements of the gentry in check and prevent them from committing excesses against the people. However, it was 'composed of the very persons who, in their local spheres, were the local government officials whom the court itself was supposed to control', and although 'most of the records of the Council have been irretrievably lost', it seems that the 'upstarts' amongst the Welsh gentry often acted with impunity.[11]

Finally, proceedings relating to riots sometimes found their way to other legal organs in London, such as the Chancery (or Lord Chancellor's High Court), the Court of Argumentations, and the Exchequer Court of Equity.[12]

Pre-Elizabethan riots, 1536-1558

The earliest riot for which there is a definite known date occurred in 1537, when disturbances broke out in and around Denbigh over disputed areas of land. This had been the source of much tension in the region for centuries and would continue to be so,[13] but over and above this reason for ructions there also 'was a feud ... between the country folk around Denbigh and the townsfolk' over the recent Acts of Union. A mob entered the town from the surrounding hinterland on a market day 'in arms, and (there) proclaimed that Welshmen were as free as Englishmen' and that as a result, henceforth they would not pay a tax known as 'stillage'.[14]

Another riotous assembly was alleged to have gathered at Holt in order to perpetrate misdeeds at some date between 1533 and 1538, following the incarceration of one Thomas Ledsham, a yeoman, who was accused of horse stealing by Thomas Hoorde. The locals turned out to protest the small holder's innocence, and they rioted when he was 'committed to the Porter's Ward in Holt Castle'.[15]

Local people also perceived injustice against some of their own at St George (Llansansior), in 1544. On 10 March Katheryn Verch Ievan ap Rys and a host of other common folk 'entered into escheat lands' which had been confiscated by a landlord when the occupier died without leaving any viable heirs, and they laid claim to tracts 'in the village of Kegedog, in the commote of Istulas', which was later called Cegidog and is now St George.[16] Two years later, on 28 March 1546, more land-related bother was purportedly initiated by Rytharch ap Gryffyth and his companions who rioted 'at Kevundy in Yale', (now Cefn Du, in the Clocaenog Forest). Sir William Norres and Thomas Massye testified that the mob 'entered premises broke and cast down the hedges and ditches for (a) distance of 60 rods or 330 yards' on their estates,[17] and a large body also made a 'forcible entry (onto) ... a parcel of ground called Segroit Parke (or Segrote, now Segrwyd)', near Denbigh, during 1547.[18]

At an indeterminate date during the reign of Henry VIII (which ended in 1547), large scale violence erupted because of a disagreement over some '40 acres (of) land ... called Harote Come (in the) commote of Kymmerche (now Llanrhaidr-yn-Cinmeirche)'. A band led by John Salysbury apparently ensured the 'forcible detention' of this pasture, and for their pains they were tried at the Court of Argumentations, which allowed them to put forward the merits of their claim against those of the complainant, Peter Hollande.[19] During this period the courts also had to preside over a case of 'riotous assembly ... at Halghton (now Halton or Halchdyn) in the parish of Hanmer' in Flintshire. In this episode supporters of the gentleman Sir Thomas Hanmer were said to have rioted in protest against the construction of a mill in the vicinity[20] and presumably this venture was instigated at the behest of their master who would have sought to eliminate any new competition for the wares produced at his own mills. Likewise, tempers flared over milling at Esclusham, not far from Coedpoeth, on 2 January 1550, when Edward ap David ap Edward 'and others' (ten of whom were named in a summons), were alleged to have undertaken the 'destruction of the mill in Esclusham and (an) assault upon the tenant [Thomas Gryndon]'. Ap Edward and his fellow defendants retorted at the Chancery in Westminster that if they had really been involved in the 'supposed ryot (*sic*)' then they should have been tried in the appropriate court, which was the Star Chamber.[21] Rioting occurred at Hanmer once again during the years that Philip and Mary were in power (1553-58) arising out of a 'dispute concerning the right to build on land' between Roger Brereton and others, and the 'unlawful assembly' caused much anxiety for both him and the rest of the propertied classes in the district.[22]

Although there were numerous reasons for rioting at this as at any other time, it seems that by the middle of the 16th century the ongoing process of 'enclosure' was causing ever greater tensions between the landowners and the poorer sections of society, and in fact it 'all but provoked revolution' at this juncture. The rich propertied class was enclosing large areas of common and waste land to which the masses had hitherto had unbridled access for grazing and other purposes, and although the new, bigger, units could be more efficiently farmed by the landlords and their tenants, many other people were being deprived of their traditional rights. As time went by and they lost more and more, they resorted to rioting to make their feelings known and to try to regain what they believed was their property, and their actions are revealed by the more extensively documented records of the Elizabethan era.[23]

Rioting in the Elizabethan era, 1558-1603

The exact dating of all the riots during this period is not certain, and so approximate dates are given hereafter (rounded to the nearest year) but it is evident that considerably more cases of riot were reaching the higher legal authorities from the 1570s onwards, and these provide a valuable insight into the type of disturbances that were occurring.

There are also records of a few earlier Elizabethan riots, the first of which was at Llansilin, south of Llangollen, in 1558, and rather unusually it grew 'out of a will dispute' between Richard Kyffyn and his kinsmen over the terms of a relative's last testament.[24] A more familiar source of friction behind a riot at Gresford in 1575 was an area of land claimed by both the landed gentleman Mr R Lloyd, and the purported leader of the mob, the Justice of the Peace, John Salesbury. The latter apparently rallied the rabble in the village and then led them in 'riots at the parish church'.[25] His central involvement in the disturbances illustrates the difficulties encountered by the Council in the Marches of Wales in retaining law and order amongst the 'higher orders', and on 11 October 1577 the Council determined that a renewed effort had to be made to rein in the troublemakers who set such a bad example to the 'lower orders', and they instructed all JPs to report to the Council within 20 days, the circumstances of any affray involving three or more men (constituting a 'Riot'), and moreover to make more of an effort 'to repress all disorders' as and when they happened.[26] In spite of the Council's appeal to the local judiciary, land-related disorders continued to break out such as the one at Nantglyn, not far from Denbigh and Ruthin, in 1578. Two factions led by Messrs ap Richard and ap Thomas ap Ievan clashed over an estate in the Vale of Clwyd, and the latter's side was charged with 'forcible entry and assaults' before the Star Chamber.[27]

During that year too, the Council in the Marches dealt with another riot in Denbighshire, where the inhabitants were regarded as 'much geeven to quarrellinge (sic)',[28] as opposed to the citizens of Flintshire who were seen by contemporaries as 'verie civile (sic)'. In the case of a riot at Chirk during 1578, the cause was not agricultural but religious, for a rabble reportedly burst into 'the house of John Edwards' and undertook grave 'disorders' for reasons 'touching (on his support for) Papistrie (sic)', or Roman Catholicism, which still had many adherents in both Flintshire and especially Denbighshire.[29]

The first disturbances of the 1580s, reverted to form, and at Flint in 1580 a mob carried out 'assaults (over) ... possession of a messuage (a house with out-buildings and land)' held by one T ap Howell of Cynfrig.[30] Similar 'riots and forcible entries (on) to land were reported in Sychnant in the township of Scrogan (or Scrugan, now known as Sgrwgan)' during 1584. Strips of land were occupied by a rabble including, *inter alia*, one Owen ap Morrice, and the target for him and his fellow rioters was a gentleman of Llangedwyn, Lewis ap Morrice,[31] which seems to indicate that another unresolved family tiff had spiralled into violence and led inexorably to the courts.

As cases of rioting stemming from realty disputes continued to burden the Council in the Marches, its members decided at Ludlow on 10 December 1585 to reiterate the need for all local sheriffs, JPs and other law enforcement officers (such as aldermen), to make a stand against 'unlawful and riotous assemblies with monstrous weapons'.[32] Indeed, travelling vagabonds and minstrels from the south of England (especially the West Country), who passed through north-east Wales and sometimes sparked off disturbances by virtue of their mere presence, were targeted by 'the parish constables of Denbighshire and Flintshire (who) were constantly at their heels'.[33] Yet the local authorities were unable to prevent rioting inspired by less obvious causes and, in any case, the gentry continued to set a bad example by quite frequently instigating violent incidents when it suited their purposes. One example was the sequence of events accompanying the construction of an industrial site at Holywell during 1589. The area around the town was already at the forefront of entrepreneurial activity, but when William Ratclyff and Samuel Fleet, a pair of London merchants and property speculators, decided to erect a lead-smelting mill 'by the river at Hallywell (sic)', not far from the lead and ore mines of 'Colchite and Ruthland' trouble erupted. Although the scheme won the approval of the Privy Council, the local squire, Piers Mostyn, was violently opposed to having 'an evil-smelling plant within a short distance of his mansion house', and his son William Mostyn JP began 'secret attempts to obstruct (the) building of (the) ... mill'. Unperturbed, the London developers erected their edifice, and as soon as it was completed William Mostyn declared publicly that it 'stode to(o) neare his father's nose (sic)' and decided to organise a 'riotous assembly ... to the number of 80' men. They made their way to the offending structure 'at night, with the object of destroying the said mill; which project was forestalled by Samuel Fleet'. But on Easter Monday 1589, they made 'further attacks ... breaking the wheel and slates belonging to same', and on 26 April they succeeded in its 'final demolition'. Yet this was not the end of the story, for there were violent recriminations between the two opposing sides, spurred on by a local 'upsurge of rural resentment towards ... Elizabethan capitalism', as well as the 'Mostyn partisans' 'attempt ... to stir up ugly feelings (among the people) by an appeal to the latent hostility (felt) against the English'. Eventually Mr Ratclyff and his associates took William Mostyn and his to a London high court over the affair,[34] and the case cannot have served to inspire any confidence amongst the central authorities that all the Welsh gentry were doing their bit to uphold law and order in their own backyards. Indeed, on at least one occasion, a Papist landowner 'attempted to fan (the) ... flame of revolt' by rousing the Catholics of north-east Wales against the English throne and, in addition, 'there was the problem of laying hands on felons and bringing them to the courts. After committing ... outrages, quite a number fled the country – the gentlemen sometimes to sea ... the common people to the woods and mountains'.[35] Nevertheless, the Attorney-General occasionally brought cases against alleged rioters and in 1589 one of these was against a mob led by Francis Kynaston and some other men of substance. They were charged by John Popham with 'intrusion into premises ... demolition ... of ... 'faire and ancyante' buildings ... (and the) destruction of ditches and quick-set hedges (sic)' at Valle Crucis, near Llangollen.[36]

At the beginning of the next decade, there was a spate of rioting over property as well. Crowds formed to oppose perceived injustices and made 'forcible entries upon lands in the forest of Rhuddallt', in Ruabon, during 1590, and not for the first time some of those charged were prominent gentlemen, including the Bishop of St Asaph![37] The Kyffyn family of Llansilin reappeared at the Star Chamber in 1590, this time in connection with 'riots and forcible entries' purportedly master-minded by them 'concerning the disputed lease of the rectory in Llansilin'.[38] A couple of miles away at Sycharth, a London-based squire, Thomas Price, apparently had to face the unwelcome attentions of a rabble amongst whom Peter Knowsley and Andrew Ellis played a prominent part. They rallied their troops in the village on 13 August 1590, and from there they headed for 'premises; threatening divers ... persons and undertaking (the) destruction of a barn ... assaults ... riotous assembly ... (and) divers other misdemeanours and affrays (sic)'.[39]

Similarly, on various plots of pasture in Bromfield, near Wrexham, there occurred in 1590 an 'assault by a large band of rioters, led by Dr Powell (another local magistrate who was) sitting in a chair directing operations'! The Justice of the Peace was arraigned along with several co-conspirators for orchestrating a 'forcible entry' onto enclosed lands, and egging the wrongdoers on to pull 'down houses, stables and out-houses', which must have been quite a spectacle from his 'director's' chair![40]

During that particularly troubled first year of the 1590s, there were further 'assaults on buildings and messuages (by the mob) ... in Esclusham',[41] but the final riot of this *annus mirabilis* had quite different origins. At Ruthin, the rioting of 1590 was a consequence of the elections currently being held in the area, and Mr E Owen of Abergele complained to the judiciary that one of their own, Mr W Wyn JP, directed the actions of an unruly horde that inflicted 'riots and assaults (upon people) in Ruthin town hall',[42] which presumably was being used as the local polling station.

During 1591 the Denbighshire custom of mob-rule was exhibited once more in Denbigh, where there was a mass 'forcible entry into a mansion ... and lands' owned by a Mr Parry,[43] and 'riots (and) assaults' also occurred at Hafod-y-wern, near Wrexham.[44] During the year after these disturbances, the ongoing difficulties experienced by the parish of Llansilin came to the fore again, with 'riots concerning the possession of advowsons (the right to be able to present oneself for a vacant benefice, or church office that yields income to the holder) of the parsonage of Llansilin'. In the serious ructions that ensued in 1592 a number of parish 'officers' were attacked by the canaille protesting against Thomas Price of Gogerddan, and as part of their campaign of intimidation they forcibly prevented the collection of tithes and even broke into the church and interrupted services.[45]

Denbigh town and shire continued to suffer 'riots and assaults' in 1593, and during that year there were riots at 'a football match arranged near the parish of Llandegla', lying between Ruthin and Wrexham. The widespread violence inflicted by those attending the game included 'assaults and ambushes', and this football-related fighting was apparently quite common during the 17th century. Indeed, football was played throughout the region (such as at Holt and Wrexham), and these fixtures often led to mass confrontations between 'players and spectators' or between teams who often prepared for a match by placing pikes and other deadly weapons within easy reach of their pitches for use if and when they could not resolve disputes over a dubious decision, foul play or a losing score-line. The crowds often followed the example set by the players, and whole groups of them often ended up before the bench on charges of rioting.[46] Other clashes that broke out in 1593 featured enclosures as the familiar focus of popular distemper, and mobs intruded 'into premises (and participated in the) ... destruction of fences (at) ... Cilcen, Trovarth and Massegwicke (or Maes-y-gwig) in the commote of Istulas', just south of Betws-yn-Rhos.[47]

1594 saw an upsurge of tension over enclosures and other contentious agricultural issues, which received a violent expression in Denbighshire and elsewhere when litigation failed to stop enclosures in various places. Indeed, although it was rare during this era for disorders to be organised effectively as part of a wider campaign (as opposed to the usual spontaneous outpourings of outraged popular feelings), in some cases 'confederacies' were formed to plan and execute a concerted campaign of direct action 'to break down the enclosures'. One example was in the area south of Llangollen 'in the lordship of Chirk' where, when the legal process had been exhausted, confederacies swung into action and groups of people swarmed onto the newly cordoned-off sectors of land 'to break up enclosures at Glyn Fechan, Llanarmon (almost certainly nearby Llanarmon Dyffryn Ceiriog), and Llangollen Fechan (Llangollen)'. The protests against Lord St John of Bletsoe were fronted yet again by local worthies, such as the Chirk JP, Mr John Edwards, and this run of riots resulted in his reappearance in the courts on the opposite side of the bench.[48] Llanarmon Dyffryn Ceiriog was the scene of a further 'forcible entry upon lands' by the hoi polloi during 1594,[49] and another part of the lordship of Chirk affected by two lots of trouble at this juncture was 'the township of Scrugan (now Sgrwgan)'. In both instances crowds took part in 'riots and forcible entries onto land' including an area known as Troed-yr-Hwch.[50]

Similar 'assaults, forcible entry (onto fields) and (also the) cutting (of) trees' was the order of the day at Ruabon in 1594, which resulted in a complaint to the Star Chamber by Mr R Lloyd of Morton.[51] Meantime, in the neighbouring lordship of Bromfield and Yale, Edward Lloyd was taking legal action against a large number of people led by Richard ap Howel, whom he accused of breaking into a tenement and 30 acres of pasture at Tyddyn Gruffuth ap

David 'in the township of Kymo (now Cymmo, near Rhewl)', as well as a mass 'intrusion (and the) ... spoil(ing) of oak trees (at) ... Koydrowg (now Coedrwg, near Llansantffraid Glyndyfrdwy)'.[52] Beyond these disturbances 'unlawful assemblies (conducted) ... riots concerning the disputed devise of lands called Dolydd in the township of Burton' not far from Wrexham, which as in so many other places involved an absentee landlord – John Trevor – who resided in London.[53] Edward Davies of Esclusham, near Wrexham, also brought a suit against John Price of Dinbrenn and the 'inhabitants of the parishes of Llangollen and Llandysilio' in 1594, this time over rioting at Valle Crucis on the outskirts of Llangollen. The defendants were charged with 'forcible intrusion ... demolition by them of walls of (Davies') ... mansion house, and wrongful carriage of stones to their own free-holds ... (as well as much) destruction of timber'.[54] The final land-related ruction of 1594 concerned a 'messuage in Trewyn', near Llanelidan, when the dastardly denizens committed 'riots (and) forcible entry' on the property of another Westminster resident, Mr S Parry.[55] Rioting during 1594 was not confined to the narrow issues of land ownership and usage, however, and at Abergele Edward Owen and a coterie of followers resisted 'the sheriff's arrest' with extreme violence. They undertook 'ambush and assault' against the representatives of authority, apparently operating in the mode of traditional Welsh guerilla fighters in 'an armed band'.[56] Even more disconcerting for the 'upper orders was an uprising at Gwytherin which involved the assembling (of) a great army at the parish church' and the execution of 'assaults' upon all those who dared to oppose them.[57] Finally for 1594, there was a riot in old Merioneth that conformed to the familiar pattern, with a 'forcible entry onto lands' owned by an absentee landlord from Kent 'in the manor of Glyndyfrdwy'.[58]

The hubbub over enclosures persisted in 1595 and, if anything, it intensified in the Llanelidan area, where there was a general 'rising of the countryside (community) ... to oppose enclosures at Trewyn'. The parts fenced in by a local landowner, Mr H. Griffith, were threatened over the course of several days, and 'unlawful assemblies (gathered) at night at Bryn Kymry (now Bryncymau farm)' southeast of Llanelidan and pulled up the fences there.[59] These types of scenes were repeated at Sgrwgan in 1595, when Tom ap Robert led 'riots, assaults and forcible entries (against) ... a messuage in the township'.[60] And 'riots and unlawful assemblies concerning ... lands' broke out near Wrexham 'in the township of Morton, in the lordship of Bromfield and Yale'.[61] A curious riot during 1595 also affected the town of Denbigh, which was reported to have been directed against its 'poor men' (who took their case to the Star Chamber), presumably because of the financial burden that their upkeep (which included the cost of a workhouse) placed on the local gentry.[62]

Enclosure rioting petered out during 1596, though there was action over 'a devise of land in Sutton' near Holt,[63] and in the following year the only riot appears to have been over 'the serving of a writ', when law officers faced 'armed resistance' at Llanbedr Dyffryn Clwyd near Ruthin.[64] Another major flare-up also occurred at Ruthin in 1598, resulting in proceedings being instigated by Owen Jones of Westminster against a multitude directed by Mr Holland, the Justice of the Peace from St George (Llansansior). Amongst a whole series of charges laid against them were those of organising and partaking in an 'armed gathering at the Great Sessions at Ruthin and rescuing prisoners' from custody, 'molesting various people with a force of 60 men', and 'other assaults, affrays and riots'.[65]

A fierce disagreement between two opposing groups took place at Ysceifiog in Flintshire too during 1598, and resulted in even more serious charges being brought at the Star Chamber, not only for the almost customary 'riots (and) assaults', but somewhat unusually also 'for murder at Skeifiog (sic)', indicating that at least one life must have been lost during the rioting there.[66]

In 1599, yet more serious trouble was occasioned at Denbigh, when the 'ordinary citizens ... (decided) to defend themselves against the (current) dictatorial attitude of urban officialdom (that was) ... inclined to act arbitrarily in matters relating to the general welfare of the community'. The aldermen and bailiffs of the town gave a 'series of orders (pertaining to legal matters to which they were supposed to attend) which were regarded as an affront by a minority of town burgesses', and the discontented element found a leader, albeit 'self-appointed ... (in) John Atkinson ... (who possessed) an uncontrollable tongue'. He made public threats to the town's big-wigs over their actions and declared his intention to organise a popular 'mutany (sic)' and, when he was arrested by the local officers, the public reaction in fact 'verged on armed revolt'. The people took to the streets and caused considerable uproar, instilling fear amongst the upper classes who were currently very wary of the pro-catholic party in the county. Indeed, they decided to forestall any possible mass uprising by charging Atkinson with treason as well as incitement to riot, and this had the desired effect of nullifying the rebellious instincts of the disenchanted folk of the town.[67]

A less ferocious, but more familiar set of circumstances, unfolded in Denbigh during 1599, with 'forcible entries' onto lands there,[68] while the last recorded riots of the century likewise were 'on ... lands in Dynyllet (now Dinkinlle) Ruabon', which were owned by the London based business man John Lancellott.[69]

The first riots of the new century were, like those at Ysceifiog in 1598, particularly bloody and resulted in at least one fatality. Early in March 1600 a 'riot and affray' occurred in Ruthin, when a gang of 'roughs' became embroiled in a spot of bother with 'John Price and others'. The local Commissioner of the Peace and the 'town officers' rushed to the scene to break up the fight and they were followed by the Deputy County Sheriff and an alderman. Prior to their intervention, one Lewis Johnes was severely wounded in the melee and subsequently died of his injuries. At the resulting trial it emerged that Price and his friends had been set upon in the street (though for what reason remains a mystery), and were only bound over to keep the peace. It seems that no-one was charged with the murder, which appears to have been a not uncommon occurrence with regard to rioting in the region.[70]

At Cefn Trevor (probably now Cefn Mawr) near Ruabon in 1600, 'an armed assembly' attacked many people and caused considerable disorder, yet the local peace officer refused to intervene to try to stop the rioting, and he was somewhat harshly reprimanded for 'failure ... to do his duty' by the Star Chamber's judges.[71]

Not long after the threat of a small scale uprising in Denbigh had passed, the town's authorities 'incurred the enmity of Sir John Salesbury (who) at one time ... had been on the terms of the closest amity' with them and the rest of the town's citizenry. He had 'vociferously championed its liberties' and their interests, especially in rivalry with Ruthin's leading family, the Thelwalls, and 'in return he had been allowed to control the appointment of aldermen and bailiffs' who were representatives of local and regal authority in the town. But in 1600 Denbigh was granted the status of a Free Borough by Royal Charter, and this afforded Sir John's placemen the opportunity to advance to become JPs, with the 'exclusive right of exercising' legal power in the town. As a result, the relationship between townspeople and benefactor 'underwent a meteoric change (and Sir John indulged himself in) ... a paroxysm of fury'. He sent a group of his retainers to attack a local gentleman, Humphrey Lloyd, who he believed to be the architect behind his loss of power and influence over Denbigh's affairs, and 'Lloyd's skull was broken' by Salesbury's club wielding thugs. Soon afterwards the embittered knight was gaoled for the assault by the new borough's officials, but on the next market day Salesbury's heavily armed crew entered the town and ransacked the stalls and 'bludgeoned ... the citizens'.[72] Some time later Sir John was released from custody and he continued to plot ways and means of restoring his former power and privilege, just waiting for the opportunity to arise for him to seize what he felt was rightfully his.

In 1601 'writ was issued for the summoning of ... Parliament' and Sir John Salesbury saw this as his chance to regain all that he had lost by standing for the County seat. 'His opponent was Sir Richard Trevor, JP (of Trefelin or Trefallyn), who had ... the sheriff, Owen Vaughan, among his political friends. Both parties ... simply terrorised those who were within the reach of their strong arm', using methods like threatening letters and mobs, and then at the end of the year Sir John decided to march on Wrexham, where polling was being undertaken, to convince the voters that they would be wise to back him. He mobilised an 'army of retainers' at Ruthin, and entered Wrexham on horseback and 'with the blowing of trumpets'. This paramilitary force marched to the church and tried to break into it, but they were confronted there by a mob of Trevorites including '80 of the toughest miners in the coalfield of Denbighshire' (the first known of many appearances by miners in riots in north-east Wales). The two sides clashed in the churchyard, and the 'the proceedings end(ed) ... in a fight with naked swords ... around the tower', which must have involved substantial bloodshed. As a direct result of this incident the election was called off and the House of Commons agreed with the Sheriff's report that it should not be re-run. Sir John's plans had catastrophically backfired and he lost his chance to sit at an even higher table at Westminster.[73]

Sir John Salesbury was not one to give up without a fight, and when it came time for the 'election of knights and burgesses for Denbigh' in 1602, his men 'attempted (to) terrorise ... the town ... with a show of force'.[74] Likewise, his opponent in these elections, Sir John Hanmer, reportedly used underhand electioneering tactics in Denbigh, raising 'confederacies, (penning) threatening letters ... (an organising an) armed assembly at the election to terrify the electors'.[75]

Lastly, in 1602, there were more of the usual 'riots, assaults and forcible entries' onto enclosed acreages in and around Llansannan.[76]

Above and beyond these known recorded riots, there were during the Elizabethan era several other disturbances in north-east Wales that are not readily dateable from existing sources. One set of 'riots and assaults' in Denbigh was purportedly the work of Sir John Salesbury's ruffians[77] (and so they may well have occurred between 1600 and 1602), while there was another case of an 'armed assembly at Wrexham (which) proceed(ed) therefrom to assault Black Park' in nearby Chirk.[78] An identical 'riotous' mob turned up too 'at the distraint (or sale in order to gain money) in lieu of unpaid charges, such as rent ... of a mare' at Llandegla.[79] And finally, in Flintshire, Mr J Griffiths, JP, of Caerwys, was embroiled with violent cohorts in 'terrorising and lying in wait and carrying out assault(s) at the (military) musters at Holywell'.[80]

Rioting in the Stuart Era, 1603-1714

Records relating to rioting for much of the Stuart years are few and far between, and those legal ones covering the early period are not generally listed chronologically. Nonetheless, in spite of this impediment, disorders in Denbighshire and Flintshire can be usefully categorised according to their underlying causes, and predictably the majority of riots stemmed from the enclosure process. There were 'riots ... forcible entries ... (and) assaults' on numerous meadows and messuages during the reign of James I (1603-25) and the case relating to those at 'Aberchwiler (or Aberwheeler) in Bodffari (now Bodfari)' was presided over by the Attorney General, Sir Henry Hobart, and involved most of Denbigh's leading officials including its aldermen, bailiffs and the mayor. Alderman John Llewellyn and his ilk were accused of instigating the trouble, and there was an additional aggravating factor of 'false imprisonment' for the court to consider.[81] When Sir Edward Coke was Attorney General, he also brought charges in a similar case in Flintshire, against Edward Morton and his accomplices from Llanasa,[82] which was where Sir John Egerton of Talacre was alleged to have suffered a forcible entry by a crowd, notable amongst whom was Mr E Morgan, JP.[83] Other riotous encroachments during this period arose at Ruthin,[84] 'on land in Bryn-y-wall' in Rhuddlan,[85] and on 'land seised (sic) of the Crown the lordship of Bromfield' near Wrexham, owned by Sir Richard Trevor.[86] In addition, at 'Frith Varchnad (possibly Ffrith between Denbigh and Ruthin) in the lordship of Denbigh', Rees ap John ap Hugh and a long list of other alleged rioters were tried for 'defacing meres and bounds and confederating to overthrow ... fences, hedges and ditches ... (and) illegal assembly carrying 'all kinds of engines and instruments and other weapons'.[87]

As well as these more run-of-the-mill riots, numerous episodes had additional interesting features, such as a 'forcible entry' at Hope that incorporated 'assault (and) destruction of enclosures (and the) rescue of sheep' that must have been enclosed along with their traditional feeding grounds.[88] One at 'Bodrigan (now Bodrhyddan near Rhuddlan), culminated in ... damage to cattle'[89] and there was 'damage to corn and cattle at Caerwys'.[90] Grain was also supposedly trampled under foot by a mob at Bodfari,[91] while at Llewerllyd, not far from Dyserth, the destruction of crops was only part of an onslaught which included 'assaults' and damage to property and led to the 'imprisonment (of people) at Flint castle'.[92] Another 'forcible dispute as to wheat sown on land (occurred) in Trerath (which may well be Trefraith, near Ysceifiog),[93] and an even more dramatic set of circumstances accompanied 'forcible entries and assaults at Bettisfield', in the 'island of Flintshire south-east of Wrexham', which had an absentee landlord living in Cheshire in the shape of Mr M Cholmondeley. The local people chased 'cattle by beating bells and brass candle-sticks', and then they concentrated their offensive on the estate's fixtures, 'carrying away timber and gates'.[94]

Other 'riotous conduct ... and assaults' in Flintshire during James I's years on the throne included a second spate of riots at Llewerllyd, near Dyserth [95] and 'riots concerning tithes at Hanmer', not far from Bettisfield.[96] Meanwhile, in Denbighshire, similar disturbances shattered the peace of Henllan on two occasions, one of which saw an armed gang stage a stiff 'resistance to a demand for (the) surrender of (their) weapons by local officers'.[97] Finally, following another forcible entry by the mob onto enclosed areas of land at Llansilin, an even greater 'riot (evolved) in anticipation of (the serving of) a warrant to arrest' on one of the 'heroes' of the crowd.[98]

It is also known that rioting raged over several nights during the summer of 1613 at 'Lyneyall', which the National Library of Wales catalogue suggests may be Llanarmon-yn-Iâl in Denbighshire. The correspondence referring to this, however, is part of the Bettisfield Park Collection, and so it seems more likely that the riots were actually just to the south-east of the houses at Lyneal, near Ellesmere, just over the border in Shropshire.[99]

Unfortunately, the available public records for the troubled decades of the Charleses and the Cromwells are very scant so that a clear picture of the rioting that must have continued during much of the remainder of the 17th century has yet to emerge.[100] But it is safe to assume that when contemporary issues affecting the masses could not be addressed to their satisfaction by peaceful means they resorted to riot, and among the key causes of bother were enclosures, food prices, and various religious, political and other disputes between different interest groups. One riot that is known about occurred at Ewloe in Flintshire during 1629, and not unexpectedly this was sparked by land enclosures. Officials of the Privy Council noted that 'some audatious persons ... (of) insolent and Rietous carrage ... (were guilty of) putting downe a new inclosure made aboute a parcelle of ... land called Ewloe Wood (sic)'. In this regard, the authorities in London repeated their condemnation of the Welsh judiciary, singling out Sir J Bridgman and Sir M Lloyd for criticism about the lack of effort being made to prevent riots breaking out and to capture rioters once they had acted outside the law.[101]

Following the disturbed years of the Civil Wars, the Commonwealth and Protectorate, the Restoration, and the Glorious Revolution of 1688, the political scene became a little less turbulent in relative terms.[102] By the end of the century the public record becomes somewhat more complete, and there are more details about rioting. The perennial problem of popular reaction to closures made life difficult for the landed classes at Denbigh in 1691,[103] and during the later 1690s the population of Wrexham became restive and they effected an 'uprising on a small ... scale' over the soaring cost of the region's staple food crop, corn, upon which an increasingly large industrialised sector of the population relied for sustenance.[104] The cost of food affected the well-being of most of the working people of north-east Wales, and fluctuations in prices, due to bad harvests or the trade cycle, were a recurrent cause of turmoil,[105] especially in the growing industrial towns like Wrexham which was already a hot-bed of social and political unrest and radicalism, with much of its populace during the 1690s supporting the restoration of the deposed catholic king, James II. This potent mix of religion and politics in fact generated considerable friction between various communities residing in the town at the turn of the century. Soon after the accession to the throne of the fervently protestant Queen Anne in 1702, the staunch Jacobins in the town jostled and harangued religious Dissenters and even 'their ministers could scarcely walk the streets with safety' during 1702. The mob further put the fear of God into them by burning straw effigies of Dissenters – which was another traditional method of civil protest often associated with rioting – and an 'effigy of Dr Daniel Williams (the non-conformist preacher) was buried',[106] an act of what must have been for many in the Dissenter camp deeply disturbing symbolism. Eventually the attacks on the religious minorities of Wrexham petered out, but rioting started there once more at the beginning of 1705. This particular bout of bustle and bluster was ostensibly engineered between two rival groups of supporters of different candidates at the forthcoming political elections, but contemporary observers note that the rabble were roused as much by local clergymen as anyone else,[107] and they undoubtedly sought to direct their venom at those who professed disparate religious beliefs.

The next recorded mob blood-letting was in the vicinity of Wrexham. The rioting of May 1709 began (like that in the 1690s), as a direct result of excessive increases in the price of corn and other staple food-stuffs that the majority of the population relied on. Following a severe and late frost during the spring of 1709, speculators in the local corn exchanges made 'ye markett (sic) to be much dearer than it would' have been under normal circumstances, and prices shot through the roof to a level three times higher than it was only one year before. Ordinary folk could not afford to buy the bare necessities at this rate, and so hungry people from all walks of life and from a wide area gathered in angry throngs and made a 'great disturbance in all ye marketts (sic)' of the district. Indeed, one diarist asserted that 'ye Mob had like (ie wanted) to kill' the traders at Erddig, Wrexham 'and several places els(e)' who they personally blamed for the sorry state in which they found themselves through no fault of their own. As the violence escalated, the authorities decided to try to prevent the rioting from snowballing and becoming a direct threat to their own property and kinsmen. The Justices of the Peace of the Wrexham neighbourhood decided that drastic action was called for, and so they ordered the local 'constables to take upon anyone ... (that) is suspected ... (of) buy (ing) corn' which would have entailed them beating up profiteers with their fists and wooden staves. And, in at least one case, the desperate members of the gentry authorised their officers to go to Chester to prevent a cart full of corn sold at the Wrexham grain market from being transferred to a vessel at the port, ready to be shipped forthwith to France. The constables apprehended the driver before he could complete his journey and they forced him to return to Wrexham, where the contents of his load were distributed to the starving Welsh poor. The authorities' pragmatic and timely intervention seems to have put a stop to the rioting and prevented the situation from getting out of hand,[108] and in this, as in many other cases, the apprehension and punishment of the rioters was relegated in importance to the preservation of the monied classes' own interests.

Popular feelings against non-conformists were running very high once more across Britain in the winter of 1709 and early in 1710, and Wrexham was affected by these sentiments more than anywhere else in the region. The emotions of the anti-Dissenting lobby were stung by the incarceration and lengthy trial of one of their leading national spokesmen, Dr Sacheverell, who was violently opposed to religious tolerance and freedom of belief. On 23 March, he was handed a meagre suspended sentence by a court in London, and on the day after this momentous decision 'great numbers of people were gott (sic) together' in the town centre of Wrexham. Orators made violent declarations against Dissenting urbanites, and on the evening of 24 March 1710 the rabble began rioting. Two witnesses to the events of that night, Hugh Roberts and Richard Jones, a pair of shoe-makers from the town, stated that at about 9*pm* some 500 or more persons assembled in 'a riotous and tumultuous manner' and then proceeded to smash the 'windows of the Dissenters' meeting house and the windows of the homes of Non Conformists', using sticks, stones and other materials. The mob paraded through the streets 'with the Beat of Drum and musick (sic) playing' for more than an hour without hindrance from the town's officers, and at the head of their column one man proudly carried 'a Barrell or Firkin (sic) advanced upon a pole with fire blazing therein'. Many of the rioters brandished 'great sticks' and used them to frighten and to beat members of the Dissenter community, and one of the ringleaders of the riots, Edward Hughes, reportedly boasted on 27 April that if he was arrested for his part in the riots the crowds would return to 'pull down ye meeting house and (they would) be the death of some of th(ose)' who worshipped within it. In fact, he remained at large after the riots of 24 March and he led further anti-dissenter riots in Wrexham one week later.[109]

At the beginning of 1711 there was an interesting twist to an incident at Galltegfa, not far from Ruthin, where some of the rioters entered the parish church and claimed the ancient and defunct 'right of Harbage'. It is not clear whether the rioters escaped the wrath of the law as those in Wrexham had done, but in a hamlet whose name means 'Gallow's Hill'[110] the rioters evidently felt anxious enough to seek out the assistance of the Church, and so they probably did not get away scot-free.

Disturbances associated with the 'Jacobite Fifteen'

In response to news of the impending ascension to the throne of the protestant Hanoverian king, George I, and in support of the revolt led by the Pretender, James Stuart, there were numerous attacks during the summer of 1715 by High Church worshippers on the dissenting communities of England and Wales.[111] This politico-religious strife affected north-east Wales, with Flintshire and Denbighshire being the main stronghold of Jacobitism in the whole of Wales,[112] and it was in the notorious trouble-spot of Wrexham, which was 'furiously attached to the Stuart cause',[113] that violence connected with 'the Fifteen' erupted most savagely and over the greatest period of time.

Not long after the new German king was offered the British crown, murmurs of discontent grew into a defiant call to arms by the middle class 'Tradesmen and some principal inhabitants of the Town', who led riotous mobs in a rampage across Wrexham (directed once more primarily against its Dissenters) on 12 July 1715. Their bad example was followed by others attracted to the rebel cause, who on 16 July stormed the Baptists' New Meeting House in Chester Street. Their minister, the Reverend John Kenrick, later described how it was 'spoiled by the High Church Rabble (who) ... pulled down the pulpit and pews ... broke down the door, and battered the windows'. After this wanton destruction the mob made its way to the Old Meeting House in the Talbot Barn on Queen Street, where the people ripped off the roof and 'destroyed ... the laths and slates and walls'. On the following day 'children and young people' joined in the mayhem, targeting the New Meeting House and doing 'a great deal of damage'. They marauded unmolested by their elders or anyone else in authority, and demolished the building's walls and timbers 'in a most violent manner'. As the turmoil spread to nearby Ruabon, its colliers and those of nearby pits at Rhosllanerchrhugog, decided to pre-empt any action that might be taken by the powers-that-be against the Wrexham rioters and they marched into the town on 18 July to lend their support and protection to the mob. Indeed, they declared that they were willing 'to assist in the Riots', and if anything they were 'positively encouraged' by the so-called guardians of law and order who both sympathised with the rioters' cause and wished to ensure that their anger remained focussed on the Dissenters rather than being shifted to themselves. Fearing for the safety of his flock, the Reverend Kenrick appealed directly to the area's leading landowner, Sir Watkin Williams

Wynn, himself a leading Jacobite, to make an appeal to the miners not to perpetrate any further attacks, and on 18 July Sir Watkin rode into the fray on his charger, admonished the miners' leaders, and forcibly 'took one of them away' with him. This prompted the rest of the miners to follow him back to their places of work, and during the rest of the day a tense calm descended on the town. A little later that evening, however, the townspeople regrouped, and under the cover of darkness they made repeated 'night attacks' on the Independent Meeting House and the Presbyterian Chapel as well as assaulting individual dissenters. These scenes continued for three nights, and then there was a lull when the rioters must have tired of their energetic activities. There was more rioting on 28 and 30 July though, and on 1 August the windows of a loyalist inn-house were smashed with stones by the Jacobins. On that day George I arrived in England in readiness for his coronation, and following this event the Wrexham Jacobite riots petered out. The people presumably took to their own taverns to congratulate themselves on their contribution to the Cause, and to toast the Pretender and to damn the usurper, and for several weeks afterwards they patiently awaited the re-establishment of the Stuart dynasty while the government set about trying to crush the Jacobite rebellion.

In conjunction with the military campaign against James Stuart's armed forces, the authorities made an effort to clamp down on troublesome elements such as those in north-east Wales, and following a wave of arrests 31 people were charged with riot at Ruthin Great Sessions on 1 September 1715. In spite of this unusually decisive action, however, on the night that the new king finally took up his throne – 20 October 1715 – there were 'great Riots and Disorders throughout Wrexham'. The 'dissenters' (celebratory) Bonfires (were) put out (by the mob), their (dwellings') windows broken, the Meeting Houses threatened, and the Mob beat at the door'. The Rev Kenrick described how 'the wild and bygotted Rabble (sic)' made 'noises like Dogs ... and treasonable songs were sung and great disorders allowed'. The authorities clearly had not deterred the populace from committing further outrages and made little effort to quash them, and the troubles even spread to Dissenter communities south of Llangollen.

Another lull followed the Coronation riots, though on 14 November 1715 there were turbulent scenes in Wrexham as the pro-Jacobite party received news that the rebels had arrived, thus-far victorious, at Preston. Indeed, one of the leaders of the Wrexham riots rode there to assure the Pretender of Wrexham's whole-hearted support for his campaign and to urge him to march into the town to gather perhaps a thousand men to reinforce his army. But, he was arrested en route to the North-West, and when word of the rebel army's defeat at Preston came through on 22 November 'this blow ... quieted the Mad and disaffected' portion of the population. In spite of this calamity many of the people of Wrexham still harboured their Jacobite sympathies though, and the day after King George's birthday (29 May 1716) they took part yet again in a 'very great riot' in the town, with the connivance of several prominent local landowners. There was also more disorder in Wrexham during July 1716, but on this occasion the military were called in by the local Magistrate using new powers granted under the Riot Act of 1715, which had been passed as the result of the nationwide disturbances of that year. The new statute allowed magistrates to read a warning to groups of rioters greater than ten in number that they must disperse peaceably within the hour or the military would be authorised to clear the area by force. In response to this new development one soldier was actually shot, but the rioters eventually were dispersed and order was restored. Indeed, as part of the anti-Jacobite repression that followed the defeat of the rebellion a number of rioters were tried and sentenced in Shropshire during 1717.[114]

Political riots from 1720

The next recorded disturbances arose in Wrexham in March 1720, when, amid rumours of an impending election, the colliers of Black Park in Chirk marched into town to demonstrate their support for their favoured prospective candidate and to confront the supporters of a rival gentleman. The two 'factions, armed with cudgels', clashed and participated in such a serious riot that the local magistrate felt obliged to read the Riot Act, which had the desired effect of dispersing the unruly mobs.[115] A magistrate and constables had to make a similar intervention at 'Llanyfydd', (later known as Llanefydd and now Llannefydd), in the uplands between Denbigh and Abergele, on 6 February 1721. Again, the reading of the Riot Act resulted in the termination of the disturbances. [116] Another politically motivated riot started in Wrexham, on 5 November 1722. From 1716, following the defeat of the Jacobite Rebellion and the resultant repression of its most active adherents in north-east Wales, the Loyalists in the town who supported the Hanoverians indulged in what one observer called 'scandalous behaviour' on each anniversary of the crushing of Guido Fawkes' 'Gunpowder Plot' of 1605. On bonfire night in 1722 they drank toasts such as 'No Popery, No Pretender', and arranged to gather at 'ye house of Phillip Phillips in the High Street ... to raise money for a bonfire to commemmorate (sic) ye Two Great Deliverances' from Roman Catholicism of 1605 and 1715. However, 'this so enraged the Jacobit(e) party in ye town ... that they got together at a distance and flung great stones ... over houses and (when it was dark) ye stones came so thick ... that the ... (Loyalist camp) could not keep round their bonfire'. The Jacobite Wrexham folk carried on their protests for several hours and, as had been the custom in the area, 'ye constables would not take notice' nor intervene while the riot raged on. Nevertheless, one man, William Griffiths, who had 'a stick in his hand', was 'dragged ... to the stocks' by a constable when he felt it was safe to arrest him, and on 6 November several people went before the local JP, Mr Ellice, who admonished them for not having assisted the constables to put a stop to the violence and he felt minded to bind them over to keep the peace. His rather lenient attitude was reinforced then by the constable's testimony, to the effect that no one was prepared to help him or his colleagues without the magistrate being present to oversee their actions, and having reflected on his submission Mr Ellice decided to take no action whatsoever against anybody.[117] This was consistent with the usual attitude of the local authorities in such circumstances and would have prevented any further recurrence of rioting as a result of any punishments that he might have dished out.

There was yet more rioting in Wrexham during 1722 over opposing candidates in the elections held during that year,[118] and a riot also broke out during the summer of 1724 at Granllyn (or Greanllyn), near Mochdre.[119]

Old Denbighshire was not alone in being afflicted by political riots around this time either, and several of those in Flintshire during the 1730s were serious, bloody affairs. At Caergwrle in April 1734, there was a ferocious confrontation between the supporters of the two leading land-owning candidates for the local parliamentary seat, Sir George Wynne of Leeswood and Sir John Glynne of Hawarden and Deeside. As the two bitterly opposed groups met within the sight of the hilltop castle at Caergwrle, one Edward Jones apparently swore 'by the Devile (sic) ... that he would kill both man (and) woman that would shout out a Glynne!' As he led a chorus of cheers for 'a Wynne!', one William Roberts shouted back 'a Glynne!' and a great struggle ensued. Witnesses reported that in the melee Edward Jones set about Roberts 'with a piece of wood' that he was carrying, and the assaulted Glynne supporter 'cryed out (sic)'. Mr Roberts in fact died of the wounds inflicted upon his person, and although the records do not say whether anyone was punished for this riot,[120] the killing illustrates the strength of feeling generated by local political rivalries and the consequent severity of the rioting. Indeed round this time several men were tried 'for a Riot at Mould (Mold)',[121] and emotions evidently were running high throughout the locality. This was particularly true in Flint, where on the final day of voting a riot broke out within the local banqueting hall, which was serving as the electoral polling station. The town's yeoman, Humphrey Lewis, was called upon to keep the peace when fighting broke out and the building was threatened with destruction, and a short while later he entered it 'with his constables a (wooden) staff in his Hand'. The guardians of the law encountered a scene of terrific tumult in which 'Sir John Glynne, Baronet, one of the (Whig) candidates at the said election, being upon the table [with many other persons who were in great Hurry, Noise and Confusion], Drew his sword and ... (cried) 'Damn you, if you don't go out I will run you through!' It appears that the yeoman and his colleagues then tried to apprehend the battling baronet, and during the struggle that followed one of the bailiffs 'fell down dead". It is not clear what fate befell Sir John after this unparliamentary display, though a trial was held during the following year.[122]

The town of Flint was also the scene of a related riot that happened on 4 May 1737. On that night a great bonfire was lit by the supporters of Sir George Wynne who wanted to celebrate his election to the House of Commons, but some time after 10*pm* things got out of hand and hordes of people engaged in a 'great Riot ... and ... fighting in the streets'. Several men from nearby Northop and Bagillt were accused of having planned the trouble and inciting the mob. They reportedly made their way that evening to 'the House of Thomas Lloyd, joiner, and presently c(a)me out again with sticks in their hands'. Thereafter they led a throng armed with 'sticks, staves or poles' to the Wynne supporters' bonfire and affronted them by chanting 'Mostyn and Glynne!' A gentleman in 'a laced Hatt (sic)', Mr Owen Lewis, is said to have responded to their taunts by defiantly waving his stick at them (in classic yobbish 'we'll have you now' fashion!), and one Robert Lloyd ran forward shouting 'God damn you, thou art for Wynne' and, an eyewitness recalled, 'at the same time he struck him a blow with a staff on the face' and Lewis fell to the ground with blood pouring from his scalp. 'Thereupon a General Battle did ensue', stated another onlooker, and in the bloody combat between the two sides there was the 'discharge of two or three guns'! Numerous people were seriously injured (some of them possibly mortally) during the riot, and several taken into custody, and it took the mobs some time to vent their anger on one another before things quietened down once again in the town.[123] Clearly, the supporters of opposing political candidates in the 18th century were roused to greater passions than their modern-day counterparts!

The Great Food Riots of 1740

Lethal though some of the electoral riots of the 1730s were the most serious riots of the whole period under consideration were those that erupted across much of old Flintshire and old Denbighshire during 1740. The harvest of the previous year had been very poor because of extremely bad weather conditions, and the situation worsened with the concomitant price fluctuations in the food grain markets. With supplies of staple crops running low in the region, already 'soaring' corn prices shot up in the springtime and by May they were more than double the level of 1739. This left many of the poorer people of the two counties malnourished and starving, and especially in the Vale of Clwyd there was 'famine and (a) high mortality' rate. As rich landowners of English stock sat by and watched the plight of the desperate local populace increase, some of the common people resorted to rioting across much of north Wales during mid-May, and by 19 May the whole of the north-east was said to be in uproar. As word of a general rebellion spread, more and more of the impoverished inhabitants of the industrial centres and market towns took to the streets and went on the warpath.

On 21 May the colliers of the Holywell area, who were renowned throughout the county of Flint for their forthrightness and steadfastness, decided to take whatever action was necessary to feed their families, and left their workplaces in droves and gathered into large groups. Miners from Mostyn and Whitford had already set them an example in the previous autumn by raiding warehouses at Rhuddlan for stocks of sugar, and now in the face of grave adversity they determined to march on the port town and seize large shipments of grain that were rumoured to be stored there. Many hungry workers and paupers joined the coal miners, and a main party of about 400 people, including iron smelters, lead miners, artisans and tradesmen, accompanied by their families, rallied and then set off for Rhuddlan. On the way a body of miners made for Mostyn Hall and there acquired 'muskets, halberds [spears fitted with axe-heads], and pikes'. Indeed, many of the colliers bore an emblem of Sir Thomas Mostyn as their uniform and called out 'A Mostyn!' as they marched. This impressive armed column proceeded through several settlements, where many of the miners chanted 'we are the Bagillt mob', and it was swelled by more and more followers as it sallied forth, including a contingent of about 300 from Denbigh and even some local yeomen. When at last they arrived in Rhuddlan on 23 May the mob had grown to between 1,000 and 1,300 people. Their leaders rallied them with speeches about the injustice of corn being shipped out of the port to Liverpool and thence to Spanish stomachs while the Welsh went hungry, and several declared that they would 'rather be hanged than starved'. They threatened that unless they were given the food that they required they would burn the town down, and when the local authorities failed to take any initiative to placate them, 'the mobs ran riot, seizing wagons (of wheat and corn), ransacking granaries (shops, houses and cellars), and threatening (the) middlemen' with violence. One of these grain dealers, Mr George Colley, had his stores of wheat and oats confiscated by the needy, some of whom threatened to blow up his and several tradesmen's houses if they did not hand over all the grain that they possessed. He then made his way into an area of marshland and in a somewhat foolhardy attempt to avoid this fate he set off a keg of his own gunpowder, which of course attracted the attention and wrath of the mob and led to them pursuing him and baying for his blood. At some point he managed to escape the excited masses by hiding in a hedge, but the rabble proceeded to his home on the 'Botryddan estate' and there they threatened to 'cut his head off and set it upon Diserth (sic) finger post and tie his guts about it'. Fortunately for Mr Colley the would-be murderers did not catch up with him, but during the Rhuddlan riot many buildings were destroyed, while only five arrests were made by those charged with preserving the peace. Moreover, as news of the rioting spread far and wide soon 'the whole countryside was ... in turmoil', and bands of marauding men caused disturbances in Cwm, Trelawnyd and St Asaph, while 400 people laid disorderly siege to Abergele with similar demands for grain. Local land owners, like William Myddleton of Chirk, feared for themselves and their property, and under pressure from the rich, on 25 May three local magistrates wrote to the Secretary of State to request military 'Aid to the Civil Power'. They reported that there were some 700 men 'with Fire Arms, Swords, Halberds, and so forth' rampaging across the countryside, and soon troops from the Chester garrison were on the move to relieve the local Sheriffs' posses and militia that had been formed in several towns. Companies of soldiers (numbering about 108 men each) were sent to Rhuddlan, Holywell and Flint to quieten these disturbed municipalities, while others made for St Asaph and Denbigh.

On 26 May the Mostyn colliers and their cohorts paraded through Dyserth, Rhyl and Prestatyn, attacking grain dealers and instigating grave 'disorders', and three days later houses were ransacked at Henllan. The rioters next trudged towards Denbigh, 'causing havoc wherever they went', taking money and crop stores, terrorising the gentry, and dispensing their own brand of 'justice' on those who they felt had wronged them. Indeed, despite the arrival of a company of soldiers at Denbigh, 'the outrageous Mobb ... (of) men, women and children' raided granaries and carted off their spoils into the surrounding hills at night time, and in undertaking these daring operations they displayed 'some rudiments of military organisation and discipline', as they studiously tried to avoid clashing with the soldiers. On 31 May, however, it seems that the raiders were spotted, and so to cover their retreat they took several hostages. A group of prominent farmers, led by a Mr Wynne of Llanyfydd (Llannefydd), assisted by troops and the men of the 'Denbigh Corporation and (the town's) Burgomasters', tracked 'ye country folk' and their captives into the nearby 'mountains ... (and there) a battle' commenced! Both the 'Denbigh Rabble' and their pursuers fired on each other with guns, and the land-owning party reported that they put about 150 of the 'ruffians' to flight by their decisive action and chased them as far as Henllan. KL Gruffydd has noted that during these bloody exchanges one of the men who confronted the mob, William Davies, was killed by them. But in addition to the Wynne supporter who 'was killed upon the spott (sic)', there were no less than 'four (men) wounded' by the crowds, and 'about 30 or 40 of the Mobb (were) desparately wounded (by their pursuers' gun-fire), some mortally'. Hence, the 'Battle of Denbigh Moor' claimed at least three lives and possibly several more, and over and above these fatalities only the intervention of Mr J Griffith, a local gentleman, prevented the summary execution of several of the captured 'Mobbility' by the farm owners. He did so by getting part of the crowd to release their prisoners, while he declared that he would take some of the rabble as 'prisoners of Warr (sic) in order that they might live to be made a publick (sic) example'. This incident forestalled further disturbances in the vicinity of Denbigh, and Mr Griffith asserted that it also prevented the full force of '700 of the Fflintshire Mobb (sic)' being railed against them.

Elsewhere, the rioting continued, and on 6 June 1740 a crowd of women forcibly requisitioned a ship-load of wheat at Rhyl, while there was also 'Mobbing' at Wrexham, where incensed citizens demanded access to the town's stockpiles of corn. However, with the arrest of several of the rioters' leaders and the continued presence of a battalion of soldiers in Flintshire and Denbighshire, in addition to the gains already made by the people, the rioting soon petered out and ended on 13 June 1740. The miners returned to their pits, their families having been provided with the food necessary to stave off starvation, and they claimed a notable 'victory' over the upper orders. The unprecedented scope of the rioting frightened the powers-that-be, and in the following weeks over 100 people were arrested, and of those tried during August 1740 a number received severe gaol sentences and seven were transported to the colonies.[124]

Political and other disturbances from the 1740s

As well as the alarums caused by the food riots in Wrexham in the middle of 1740, there was another fearful disruption of the town's life at that juncture over the concurrent elections. The familiar pattern unfolded as fighting broke out between two rival groups of people supporting the local landowners Sir Watkin Williams Wynn and Sir John Myddleton, and some contemporaries thought that the riots engineered by gentry from Holywell who supported the latter candidate.[125] Further hubbub connected with Sir Watkin cropped in 1745, at the time of the second Jacobite Rebellion headed by 'Bonnie Prince Charlie'. Tradition has it that several Jacobin gentlemen of Flintshire attempted to make contact with the Young Pretender at Manchester and Derby, and that Sir Watkin was preparing to raise an army of 1,000 men from the shires of Denbigh and Flint to back his cause. The panic spread to London, where there were rumours that Chester might fall to the Welsh rebels, but the only action that occurred in the region during this attempt on the throne was the arrest of some rabble rousers who were busy fomenting trouble in the Hawarden area.[126]

Further Jacobite-related bother manifested itself in Denbigh during the 1750s, where 'quasi-Jacobite ... Methodist' preachers were at the root of some 'scenes of great tumult and disorder'. The strangers were not well received, on several occasions being 'pelted with stones and turf, tossed into rivers ... captured ... and subjected to all kinds of humiliations'.[127] Across the county boundary at Threapwood in Flintshire there were similar instances of 'disorder and irregularity' during the summer of 1753, where 'asylum' was granted by the residents to 'many disorderly persons', much to the chagrin of the local lords of the manor.[128]

In the wake of more foul weather and bad harvests during 1757-58 grain prices again rose dramatically, and there was a recurrence of rioting and pillaging of crop stores in various Welsh towns.[129] Although records for north-east Wales at this time are scant, it is quite likely that places such as Denbigh, Rhuddlan and Wrexham were affected, though to a lesser extent than during 1740, and in 1767 it was said that the poor of Hawarden were 'Starving, Riotous and Hanged'.

The miners of Wrexham were active once more in 1776, the year of the American

Revolution, and while their cause was not revolutionary it was anti-English, centring on the management's employment of English labourers in their mines. Such protests became commonplace as the pace of industrialisation and the demand for coal and men to mine i grew, and the rising of the Wrexham colliers 'in riotous and tumult manner' on 10 October 1776 proved very 'difficult to handle',[130] and it was the first of many overtly nationalistic industrial riots that followed in later years.

Miners, who were commonly condemned by their social 'betters' for spending their 'leisure hours, and the Sabbath in particular, in the public houses, in noise and riot', were also at the heart of disturbances over food shipments from Flintshire during the spring of 1778, when supplies were needed to feed the hungry of the county after another poor harvest They forcibly prevented the export of grain from the port of Flint, and again their rioting achieved the limited objectives that the people had set.[131]

Disturbances following the French Revolution, and during the French Revolutionary and Napoleonic Wars

In 1788, after one of the worst winters of the 18th century, the price of wheat rose sharply and sparked growing unrest in Flintshire and Denbighshire. The threat of more food riot instilled fear amongst the upper orders because they were 'the most dangerous (type of popular disturbance' to deal with effectively, for when the population were utterly desperate they often directed their unbridled anger and ferocity at those in high places. This is exactl what happened in France during the summer of 1789, and following the overthrow of the ancien regime there, those in positions of power in Britain were gravely uneasy and hope that a similar fate would not befall them. As the hungry people of north-east Wales resorted to strikes and rioting during the summer months of 1789, many of the landowners and industrialists of the region prayed that they would not gain momentum and induce a mas uprising. 'In the district stretching from Holywell to Oswestry thousands of colliers were ou in search of bread', and with their discipline and organisational skills they rallied groups o 'weavers … knitters, smiths, iron-smelters, sailors, agricultural labourers and so on' in the main towns. At Denbigh 'waggons (carrying grain) were stopped (by the mob), boats wer destroyed, and 'gentlemen of the first rank' were insolently called upon … to lower their rent (to what the people deemed a 'fair' rate) or take the consequences!' The rioting was bot widespread and well executed, with the mob placing sentries at various points in the 'liberated' town and controlling all passage into and out of it for some time, and the rabbl even advanced on the Militia Headquarters and threatened to take its weaponry from it.[13] This must have seriously worried the monied classes in the town and its neighbourhood, an the Home Secretary, William W Grenville, declared that such disturbances were only 'on the pretence of the high price of corn' and were actually politically motivated. Just after the fal of the Bastille in Paris the people of Wrexham similarly took to the streets in what wa described as a 'seditious spirit', led by 'the colliers, miners and other persons of the description', and as the position deteriorated in August 1789 the town magistrates requested military assistance. Secretary Grenville reassured them and the anxious 'principal' citizens of the town that soldiers commanded by Lord Burford would stop 'any mischief' and seek out and apprehend any 'Insurgents who do not confine their views to the pretended subject'. Three troops of mounted Dragoon Guards arrived soon after from Manchester, and the government's estimation of the seriousness of the situation can be gauged by its unprecedented offers of 'Rewards ... (for) information (that afford) the seizing and bringing to punishment of the ring-leaders of the conspiracy', as well as the granting of the 'King's Pardon' to any informant who may have had a hand in the proceedings. This had the desired effect of quieting Wrexham, but three months later the 'middle order of people' still feared the possibility of 'revolt' and they decided to establish 'a Body (of men), to secure, in future, private Property ... (and to) oppose every tumultuous body'. Their new Association was to number 140 men and to be maintained 'till the Mob is brought to a more peaceable Temper'. It remained ready for action throughout the autumn of 1789, when the unrest in the area eventually died down.[133]

Although the Jacobite cause had withered elsewhere by the 1790s, disturbances relating to it were still a feature of life in Wrexham.[134] But the main trouble early on in that decade stemmed from another long-standing point of contention between the common people and the upper classes, namely enclosures.

With the growing demand for food during the French Revolutionary Wars, in which Britain became entangled from 1793, land owners began to see the potential value of areas of upland, marshes and other tracts that had not been cultivated intensively before, and they took advantage of the wartime situation to lay claim to them and to fence them off and incorporate them into their own estates. This angered many of the ordinary folk of Flintshire, whose numbers had rapidly grown over the course of the 18th century, with the result that they suffered from an ever increasing 'land hunger'. When the landed gentry began to fence-in large areas during the spring of 1793, groups of the less well-off decided to oppose their encroachment onto their traditional common grazing lands, and at Hope large bodies of people led by a local labourer, Thomas Jones, pulled dawn some newly erected fences that had isolated around 3,500 acres of land. He was arrested swiftly in order to send a message to other would-be troublemakers, especially in view of the wartime situation, and he was incarcerated in the county's own 'Bastille' – Flint Gaol. On 20 April, Richard Roberts, a yeoman of Hope, organised fund-raising efforts and sent for manpower from Kinnerton, Brymbo, Shordley, and elsewhere, determined to break him out of captivity. On the following day about 200 men met at nearby Pontblyddyn and in scenes of uproar obtained a free half-pint of ale each, provided by nearby hostelries and paid for by 'subs' from the farming community. They duly set off and arrived at the coast after a ten mile trek by mid-day, where they laid seige to the prison with clubs and stones and broke most of its windows. In the face of this onslaught two of the crowd's leaders were granted entry and they whisked Jones out of his cell and the gaol. The jubilant throng returned via Penyffordd, where more fences were burned, and the following morning, 100 men were induced by rallying speeches and free beer to prepare for more mayhem. At the *Red Lion* in Hope, however, they were confronted by three JPs, and one of them, the Rev Richard Williams of Mold, ordered them to disperse. When they refused he read the Riot Act but this had no effect either, and about 150 men engaged in 'great ... Riot in the Hope and Mold neighbourhood'. Indeed, Richard Roberts called for the poor of Hope to rise up in revolt against their masters, and one anxious landowner, Sir Roger Mostyn, worried that the rioters were acting on much more 'than the local grievance of an inclosure (sic) ... because they are incited to murmur against all order'. He demanded 'the severest check' be applied to them by the authorities, and not long after the enclosure riots began a 'party of the Warwickshire militia' arrived in the area to restore order. They guarded the homes of the JPs who had called for their assistance, and it was not long before they had 'secured some of the Ring leaders'. As a consequence the rioting petered out, and by the time that the Warwicks were replaced by the Westmorland and Cumberland Regiment in the middle of May 1793 the situation had settled dawn. Yet the cause of the dispute had not been eliminated, and unrest simmered beneath the surface, so much so that, when some of the enclosure rioters were tried, a panel of judges pardoned and freed them all from Flint Gaol by 1794, principally because of their belief that if any of them were punished further then the people may rise once more and 'pull down all the rest of the inclosures (sic)' in the Mold district.[135]

The fears of the élite were shared in Denbigh and Ruthin at this time and public meetings were arranged during 1794 to organise volunteer militia forces led by some of the law-abiding 'middle orders'. Like the unit that had been set up in Wrexham in 1789 these were perceived as essential for preserving internal security during a period of unprecedented danger to the nation, and the leading residents of Denbigh were prepare to pay 100 men £10 each to provide them with protection from rioters.[136]

The rioters renewed their activity across the two counties in 1795, but for familiar reasons rather than the new revolutionary ideas that had engulfed France. In many districts the price of bread was double that of 1794, and the poorer people living in north-east Wales' most industrialised communities were very badly hit by the increase. At the start of 1795 'huge gangs of colliers scoured the North-eastern coalfield' of east Denbighshire and Flintshire for food, and 'large mobs frequently assembled'. On top of the rising rents, prices and taxes caused by the war, and the increasing pressures on small farmers' land and employment prospects because of both the fighting and the ongoing process of agricultural mechanisation, the threat of starvation pushed many ordinary folk beyond the limits of their endurance. Encouraged by Methodist ministers who were 'said to have spread sedition among the working classes', especially in Denbighshire, the government provided the spark to light the touch paper and set off another wave of riots, in the shape of the Navy Act and the Militia Act, which were passed on 5 March 1795. Under the terms of the former statute, local magistrates were given the power to select men from their localities for wartime service in the Royal Navy, and Denbighshire was obliged to provide 75 men for such duty. The people of the county were already generally ill-disposed towards their local JPs, and with the news of the proposed impressment of some of their sons the people determined to resist. Their resolution was reinforced by the introduction of the Militia Act which was designed to bring about the formation of additional auxiliary units tasked with 'internal defence'. But many people believed that once the men had been enlisted in these forces they would be surreptitiously sent to the Continent to fight, and one contemporary observer, Thomas Hanmer, criticised the authorities because he felt that the Act had not been properly explained by the magistrates and that it had been misrepresented in the newspapers which had said 'that the Justices ... were to send all persons that could be best spared out of each town'. Hence, on 1 April 1795, a dozen or so groups of people from Denbigh and 'from the district', numbering about 500 in all, congregated as 'a very considerable Mob'. They were 'lead (sic) by ill-designing persons ... (and) armed with large sticks, and bludgeons' and, as in 1789, they displayed their military acumen by taking up strategic positions about the town, such as the medieval walls and gates, in preparation for the arrival of the local magistrate, John Lloyd. Several of the 'heroes of the crowd' made speeches about natural justice and 'Jacobin democracy', and 'some of the Ringleaders of the Mob threatened' the Establishment. John Jones, an educated and eloquent farmer of Aerdden, delivered a fine political oratory about John Lockes' *Rights of Man* and the principles of the American Revolution, notably 'no taxation without representation'! This was a truly forward-looking, if not a seditious, viewpoint for the times, and some gentlemen listening said that 'much seditious and disagreeable language' was used. Following the lead of their speakers, the crowd confronted some of the gentry and the owners of larger farmsteads who had been enrolled as special constables by John Lloyd, but they could not prevent him, a fellow magistrate and the Rev Clough from being captured by the crowd and 'imprisoned' for a while at the *Crown Inn*. There they were forced by threats of violence to sign statements to the effect that they would not implement the Militia or Navy Acts in Denbigh now or at any time in the future, and that in addition they would pay compensation of five shillings to each member of the mob 'for their loss of time' spent in having to riot to get justice! Having gained these concessions from the defeated authorities, the people lifted their stranglehold on the town and dispersed back to their small holdings, dwellings and workplaces, but similar disturbances soon arose elsewhere in Denbighshire and Flintshire and John Jones of Aerdden 'seems to have taken an important part in a number' of them.[137]

In Flintshire, 300 men were required for service in the militia under the dictates of the new Act, and on the day after the Denbigh riot ,Thomas Griffiths of Rhual, between Gwernaffield and Mold, noted that 'different mobs in considerable numbers, have repeatedly assembled in different parts (of the district)'. The terms of the Act would have incensed the already enraged crowds who had been rampaging for some time, as in Denbighshire, because of the high cost of corn that left them on the brink of being famished. The current unavailability of troops also contributed to their willingness to riot, and 'the greatest violence used was at Mold', where hordes of hungry people battered down the doors of warehouses full of corn destined for Englishmen in Cheshire and Lancashire, forcing the traders to sell their grain to them at what they deemed to be a 'fair price' – which would have been much lower than the current market rate. As in many other cases the multitude were led by colliers and other miners (from nearby lead, zinc and copper mines), and the rioting grew to be so severe that the gentry feared for their safety and pressed the magistrates to call in the military which arrived to disperse the Mold assemblage and restore law and order.[138]

In the meantime, a host of people who had participated in the Denbigh riot were heading north for the port of Rhuddlan to confiscate grain supplies for themselves and their kinsmen, and this 'great body of lawless Banditti' caused much disorder on arrival in the town.[139] A week or so later, on 10 April, about 400 people 'armed with long sticks with a sharp hook ... attached to the end' vented their anger and 'ill will' over both the high price of corn and the recent enclosure of expanses of common land in a 'serious Riot' at Abergele. The rabble were reported to have 'behaved very riotously', wounding several people who crossed their path, and in the absence of any soldiers in the locale the requests of local gentlemen for the Riot Act to be invoked were dismissed and, as elsewhere, it appears that no arrests were made nor any of the rioters punished.[140] At the end of the month, the upper orders in Denbigh, not for the first time, were gripped by fear as a rumour spread that a mob of 4,000 people (probably an exaggerated report of the crowd at Abergele, increased by an order of ten), were preparing to overrun the town. The Rev Clough, who had been manhandled by the mob only a few weeks before, took it upon himself to demand military assistance, and the Duke of York obliged with 70 men of the Somerset Cavalry who were stationed in Denbigh for some time. In addition, the Cardigan Militia were put onto alert in Ruthin, and troops were posted later in Mold and Holywell. Indeed, the better-off citizens of Mold soon followed the example set by their neighbours in Ruthin and Denbigh and arranged for the creation of their own military force, the Flintshire Yeomanry Cavalry, for the purpose of internal defence, while the authorities in Holywell contemplated the construction of a new workhouse as a means of placating the poor of their parish. [141]

Following the introduction of military garrisons into some of the most troublesome towns, the atmosphere became a little more settled, and on 14 August 1795 seven men received sentences of 2-3 years imprisonment or fines for their part in the Denbigh riot (although a year later several prisoners escaped from the County Gaol at Ruthin).[142] But, in spite of the apparent return to normality, the common people's grievances had not been adequately addressed and trouble was brewing beneath the surface in some areas over the unaffordable cost of many scarce staple foodstuffs. In November 1795, the lead miners of Talargoch, near Dyserth – who were renowned for their militancy – led a mob of hungry Flintshire folk to Rhuddlan. There they created rowdy scenes and forcefully expressed their political opinions to those who had gathered to listen, after which they prevented the export of grain in ships that were docked at the port and then helped themselves to the harvest.[143] Early in 1796 they repeated their riotous raiding on Rhuddlan, and at least two troops of cavalry from Mold and Holywell were required to restore the peace.[144] It seems that the mob may have taken advantage of this situation, for Mold itself was struck by 'frequent ... illegal proceedings' perpetrated against grain dealers and their stores, and the town's magistrates are said to have allowed the rioters a free hand. Predictably, they were led in at least some instances by 'potters and colliers from the Hawarden side' of the county.[145] In addition, groups of women in Hawarden took to the streets and ambushed several waggons carrying grain and distributed quantities of it to the villagers. In this case, however, the authorities did act , and two of the women arrested were tried and sentenced to transportation.[146] There was more rioting over the Militia Act during 1796 and these disturbances were the final ones recorded in the 18th century.[147]

The first disorders of the new century broke out for familiar reasons, with the severe winter of 1799-1800 resulting in grain shortages in Flintshire and Denbighshire. By December 1800 Sir Roger Mostyn alone was feeding '3,000 mouths ... (of the) burthensome (sic) ... poor' on his estates,[148] and the month before that there were reports that pikes were being distributed by rabble rousers to the population, amongst whom 'there was talk of 'insurrection' in the industrial regions' of north-east Wales. At the beginning of 1801 large crowds armed with pikes and other formidable weapons rioted in Holywell and Denbigh over the exorbitant price of corn and their deteriorating living conditions and over 100 people seized stores of barley at Towyn. On 27 January troops arrived in Holywell and Denbigh to put a stop to the conflagrations there, but in spite of the activities of the military, republican sympathies were expressed in rebellious Wrexham, and violence flared up in nearby Rhosymedre, and at Bagillt, not far from Holywell.[149]

Over and above the rioting caused by such issues as food shortages and the poor quality of life endured by most of the populace, the considerable industrial tensions present in Holywell during the 1800s were manifested in violent strikes. Although the heartland of North Wales' industry does not appear to have been much affected by Luddist machine wrecking, a dispute at Wilkinson's lead-works in Buckley led to an incendiary attack in December 1802. This new tactic of protest, sometimes associated with other forms of civil dissension including rioting, became more and more common as the century wore on, and there was a spate of such attacks on farms at Henllan in January 1809. The growing influence of Methodism by the 1810s seems to have had something of a calming influence on the region though, and the only other riot recorded during the war years was one over enclosures at St George, on 19 December 1814.[150]

Riots during the post-war depression

Following the final defeat of Napoleon Bonaparte, Great Britain was hit by prolonged bouts of economic recession, and in 1815 the long suffering people of Denbigh replicated their actions of twenty years before by marching on the town and imprisoning the local JPs until they agreed to accede to the demands of the mob. In spite of the presence of a dozen constables (who included some of the famous Bow Street Runners, three of whom also served in Mold during the 1800s), the magistrates once again were obliged to pay compensation to the people for the time that they had had to spend rioting (probably over increased rents or other pressing local issues). Further disturbances broke out over land disputes during 1815, and there were also a series of incendiary attacks along the border with England.[151]

In 1816, a quarrel over fishing rights led to violence between two groups of men at Northop, where more than 150 nets and stakes were destroyed. But the most serious rioting of the early postwar slump occurred in Wrexham during 1816. There the colliers walked out over changes that resulted in a deterioration in their working conditions, and in October 1816 they confronted units of the local Wrexham Yeomanry Cavalry before being dispersed back to their pits. Colliers undertook similar disturbances at the Ffrwd pits near Brymbo during May 1817, and again in Wrexham that September.[152]

As the economic depression deepened, unrest spread across England and Wales, and in the summer of 1819 it culminated in the bloody and infamous 'Peterloo Massacre' near Manchester. Mindful of the concurrent 'political excitement' exhibited by the working class of the two counties, the Yeomanry Cavalry were put on stand-by in the major towns, and on 10 December cavalrymen of the Royal Maylor were called in to Bagillt to put down a riot there. The Bagillt miners had been seeking an increase in their pay to compensate for the rising cost of living, and it appears that unemployed colliers from Brymbo arrived in the Holywell area in the hope of obtaining work in their pits. This provoked the Bagillt men to go 'up in arms' against them and when the cavalry arrived on the scene they were stoned by the wives of the Bagillt colliers. However, the military soon restored order and dispersed the miners, who returned to work without gaining any increase in their wages.[153]

During the 1820s, recurrent trade recessions had a 'serious (detrimental) effect upon wages (that) led to frequent scenes of turbulence and rioting' in north-east Wales, and this was probably at the heart of the trouble in Holywell's mills in March 1822 that included a number of incendiary attacks. [154] At that juncture there was also a 'general panic' in the local markets and grave apprehension amongst the upper classes that 'anarchists' who were spreading the 'pernicious doctrines ... (of) Payne, Cobbett and Carlisle' could arouse the passions of the workers and instigate riots.'[155] But in spite of such talk about sedition in the air, the main causes of large scale violence continued to be parochial, as exemplified by a disturbance orchestrated by the Halkyn miners in December 1822. They walked out in protest at the management's arbitrary introduction of an 'improved system' of working practices centred on a new shift rota devised by a Cornish engineer, John Taylor. The miners made their feelings known about his foreign thinking in no uncertain terms by rioting, and once again the militia were utilised by the authorities to restore normality to the area.[156] 'Their sight and presence ... (was often) a strong deterrent in a community highly prone to industrial dispute and civil unrest', but when the people saw that they were being backed into a corner over an issue about which they felt very strongly they were prepared to riot and to take the risk that the militia might be called on to lend aid to the civil power, as they were in 1825-26 when colliers rioted in Holywell, Hawarden and Mold. Indeed, in spite of the Flintshire Yeomanry Cavalry's garrison at Mold, rioting broke out there in March 1826 following an attempt by local pit managers to introduce the Cornish Shift System of working 8 hours in 16 (as opposed to 6 hours in 18), which had caused so much trouble at nearby Halkyn. The Mold colliers of Bromfield and other pits responded with a demand for an unprecedented six-hour-a-day shift pattern, and when it became clear that the management would not make any concession to them the miners rioted. On 6 March the town's Yeomanry were sent to suppress the riots, but they became so widespread and severe that the authorities had to send for reinforcements from Holywell and two troops of the Royal Maylor Cavalry (which caused a major panic among the property owners of Wrexham who feared that the mob would take advantage of their vulnerability and rise there). The disturbances in and around Mold were described as 'most serious rioting' and must have been quite bloody, for the cavalry were out on patrol for 12 days, four of which they were involved in clashes with rioters, and there were still ructions going on as late as 26 March. Indeed, during April and May of 1826 Northumbrian colliers employed at the nearby Coed Talon pit went on strike and rioted, and once more the cavalry had to ride out to crush the felons. Thereafter, the leading inhabitants of Mold requested and received a reinforced garrison for the town, and this enlarged military force was retained until 1827 to deter 'the malcontents of the County' of Flintshire from undertaking further rioting.[157]

Discontent was not confined to Flintshire at that time either, for on 13 and 22 June 1826 there was 'riotous and tumultuous assembling together of 20 and more persons' in the centre of Denbigh. The rioters attacked various properties including an inn owned by one Judith

Woods, which was 'broken and destroyed' by the mob and cleared of much of its fixtures and fittings. The crowd also laid siege to a nearby house and with 'their hands and feet ... stones and other missiles ... staves, sticks and other weapons broke and destroyed' its contents or took them away with them. At the hearings that followed during the summer it became clear that the perpetrators were 'then and now unknown' to the authorities and so it appears yet again that the rioters got away home-free.[158] The same was very probably true of the miners who partook in violent, nationalistic demonstrations against the employment of English labourers at pits in Halkyn and Leeswood near Mold in 1826-27, and of those who carried out incendiaries on farm buildings across Flintshire in January 1828.[159]

The Crisis of 1830-32

The years 1830 to 1832 witnessed the greatest rise in social and political tensions across Britain since the beginning of the Civil War in 1640, and although D W Howell has asserted that in Wales there was no 'widespread revolt in the autumn and winter of 1830-31' as there was in some parts of England, there were major disturbances in north-east Wales during this period.[160] One of the main causes of popular unrest was the ongoing process of agricultural mechanisation that was threatening the prospects of many small holders, and the severe early winter and poor harvest of 1830 added to their difficulties. This spurred on a campaign of attacks on agricultural reformers and their newfangled machinery across southern England and some of the Midlands in 1830. And these 'Swing Riots' (so-called because of the fictional character of Captain Swing, who represented the traditional farmer and his old-style reaping methods) had a 'few poor followers in Flintshire'. Like their counterparts in England, they engaged in disorder and in March 1830 burned down hay 'stacks and out buildings' across the county, then undertook a concerted campaign of destruction through the winter of 1830.[161]

Over and above this agriculture-inspired rumpus, tensions were rising throughout industrial Flintshire and Denbighshire during 1830, the year in which the first consolidated British trade unions were formed. A month after the founding of the Friendly Associated Coalminers' Union in Lancashire, a lodge was opened at Bagillt, and during the autumn 'menacing crowds' composed mainly of miners 'appeared periodically near the houses of the principal mine-owners' in both counties. Indeed, there was daily industrial strife centred on the coalfields and iron-producing districts (which had been in relative decline since the year before), and when organised industrial rioting swept across England in December 1830 north-east Wales was affected also.

Officials of the new colliers' union planned to bring the 'coalmen' of Flintshire out on strike for better wages as part of a wider campaign, and on 20 December the Hawarden miners downed tools and demanded more pay. Their managers agreed to an increase provided that other pits in the vicinity followed suit, and so union representatives travelled to various mines in the area to try to open up union branches in them and gain concessions from their owners. On Christmas Eve, following negotiations with union officials, the Hawarden miners were

assured that they would get their pay-rise in the New Year and so they returned to work. On the following day, however, Mr William Eyton of Leeswood, near Mold, had his Christmas celebrations ruined when a mob of miners from his pit at Coed Talon, many of whom were from Northumbria, demanded a pay-rise that matched that promised to the Hawarden colliers. On 26 December the very ruffled Mr Eyton begged for the Flintshire Yeomanry Cavalry in Mold to 'repress ... tumult' in the district, and Sir Stephen Glynne of Hawarden also requested a detachment of troops from Chester Castle. His plea was rebutted, however, because of the fears of higher authority that the city of Chester itself may be threatened if a rumoured 'national turn-out' of miners materialised on 27 December. Thus encouraged, the Coed Talon coal workers gathered at Mold on that day, and there they were joined by 400-500 miners and brick workers from Hawarden who were said to be in 'rebellious mood'. They marched in a large column to Buckley, where another 100-plus colliers and iron-workers swelled their ranks, and then proceeded to the Ffrwd pit at Brymbo. As this mass of malcontents advanced nearer to Wrexham and set off alarm bells there, there was also panic in Holywell because of rumours that another party of miners had gone through Sychdyn en route to it. In this highly charged atmosphere, a messenger was despatched to Hawarden by one concerned landowner 'to ascertain the movements of the rioters', and he was followed close-by by the Lord Lieutenant of Denbighshire, Sir Watkin Williams Wynn (whose forebear had intervened in the Wrexham riots of 1715), and his men of the Denbighshire Yeomanry Cavalry. Special constables were sworn-in at Wrexham, Rhosllanerchrhugog, Denbigh, Gredington and other places, and Lord Kenyon put his men on alert around the town of Wrexham.

As all this hustle and bustle was going on, the miners assembled at the Ffrwd pit on 27 December before moving out in groups to mines in the Brymbo area including Southsea and Coedpoeth, and several around Wrexham such as Rhos, Ruabon, Plas Madoc, Cefn Mawr and Chirk. At all these shafts new volunteers pledged themselves to the cause, some of them being attracted by the idea of higher wages, while others wanted to protest about their 'very hard and unjust' working conditions, or about the widely-loathed 'Truck System' of payment in-kind or by special tokens (which had to be spent at company shops) in lieu of money. Having gathered a mass of supporters the miners organised a meeting near Rhos mill for the following day, in order to address all the issues raised by the miners and to decide upon a plan of action. When they turned up on 28 December the coal miners were bolstered by quarrymen from Cefn and about 500 colliers from the Flint area, and in all the throng totalled upwards of 4000 people. By this time the Lord Lieutenant had been appraised of the miners' intentions, and he arrived at Rhos with about 400 cavalrymen, policemen and special constables. Standing nearby Sir Watkin heard the miners' leaders berate the Truck System and call for a march on the British Iron Company's 'Truck' or 'Tommy Shop' at the Acrefair Iron works, and he declared that he 'had some sympathy with the men's demands' and would try to broach the subject with the Works' owners on their behalf if they would call off their march and disperse in an orderly fashion. There are conflicting accounts of what happened next at Rhos, but the events that unfolded resulted in a quasi-battle.

Sir Watkin Williams Wynn, Bt (in the uniform of the Royal Denbighshire Rifle Corps), c1825.

It seems that the colliers' leaders were prepared to accept Sir Watkin's offer and asked for those assembled to leave the area, but some of the embittered workers' wives refused to move and began to throw stones at the Yeomanry, who were there 'to try to terrify (or cow) the people'. At this point some of Major E L Lloyd's heavily outnumbered troopers apparently became restive and 'charged' towards the crowd, which led to even more stoning. The local magistrate, Richard Lloyd, quickly read the Riot Act, but 'the crowd called out in derision 'Read it in Welsh!' '. Some of the mob then vented their anger on the representatives of authority for a time, though they eventually melted away before Sir Watkin had to take any further action. Shortly afterwards, he decided that his party should withdraw and his cavalrymen set off. En route the soldiers were obliged to pass the cinder heaps at Gutter Hill where they were jeered by the mob who were now atop these stacks of ready-made ammunition. One youth threw a lump of slag at one of the soldiers and hit his horse. The animal reared, and the panicking cavalryman fired a shot towards his assailant, narrowly missing his head, and then 'a pitched battle' ensued. The security forces were showered with thousands of projectiles and forced to retreat in short order, and 'two or three of the Denbighshire yeomanry ... fired before being ordered to do so'. Sir Watkin set about trying to restore discipline among his men while the cavalry made another charge, which resulted in the arrest of one of the leaders of the mob, Dafydd 'Dwr' Jones. Before events could escalate, however, Sir Watkin ordered his men to release the self-styled son of Glyndwr, and he publicly and 'severely reprimanded the two troopers (who had opened fire on the crowd) for their silly and dangerous act'! Thereafter, the miners' leaders were able to convince the people to leave before there was more bloodshed, and they made for home claiming victory in the 'Battle of Cinder (or Gutter) Hill'.

On the next day, Sir Watkin, accompanied by Captain Morris, went to the Acrefair truck shop where they were cheered by large crowds as they took the communities' grievances to the works manager, Mr Wood. Sir Watkin 'implored (him) ... to abolish the shop', especially when he found out at first hand that it gave short measures of various goods, and eventually Mr Wood begrudgingly agreed to meet with the strike leaders to try to resolve the issue at the *Wynnstay Arms Hotel* in Ruabon on the following day. The masses outside the shop were deeply upset that Sir Watkin had not managed to have it summarily closed down, however, and as disorders broke out the Riot Act was read once more by the local magistrate. This had the desired effect and the people dispersed shortly afterwards.

On 30 December, at the appointed time and place, the two sides in the dispute met. But Wood refused to countenance any concession to the strikers' demands and Sir Watkin left the hostelry in disgust at his attitude. At this point the ranks of miners and their supporters outside the *Wynnstay Arms* got wind of what they regarded as Wood's 'broken promise', and one of his colleagues 'annoyed the colliers outside the inn by laughing and sneering at them through the window'. He should have known better. This childish behaviour stretched the colliers' patience beyond endurance and a good number of them immediately barged into the pub with cries of 'Blood or Bread!'. Wood, fearing for his life, drew his pistol and shot one of the strike leaders, Dan Davies. Evan Evans then tackled Wood to the floor and, assisted by several of his comrades, proceeded to beat the manager senseless. The miners then dragged the unconscious man out into the streets of Ruabon, along which he was pulled for about 50 yards and was 'struck, kicked and stamped upon', noted a witness, 'with a brutality that makes one

An officer and trooper of the Denbighshire Yeomanry Cavalry, c1831 by R Simkin.

shudder!'. One of the mine owners who had joined Wood at the *Wynnstay*, Mr Exuperius Pickering, was likewise beaten up, and then forced by the angry coalmen to guarantee his workers pay of 3/- a day. After his signature was extracted he fled with a Mr Parry from 'the fury of the mob (which) was such that no person was safe'. After picking up the battered Wood, they made a quick dash along the streets and found temporary sanctuary in one of the houses nearby. Miners broke into it and others in search of them, but hiding in a bedroom – two of them behind a door and one of them under the bed – they fortuitously escaped detection. Later that evening, under the cover of darkness, they eventually slipped away, with Woods swimming across a river dressed as a woman!

The day after these colourful and violent events the miners gathered again in Rhos 'armed with bludgeons' and they resolved to hold another mass meeting on the morrow. Sir Watkin Williams Wynn learned about this, and on the 1 January 1831 he attended their rally, and to resounding cheers he informed them that Mr Woods had been sacked and that the Acrefair truck shop was now closed. The colliers still had other demands, however, and it was announced that their employers in Flintshire and Denbighshire had agreed to meet them as long as the mine owners in neighbouring Shropshire would apply the same conditions to their pits. The strike leaders therefore proposed to march towards Oswestry, and on 3 January the colliers set off for the town, led by a constable. They passed by the shafts at Acrefair, Cefn and Black Park, and caused fresh turn-outs and some disorder there. Then, on arrival at Newbridge, the crowd of about 2,000 took time out for a rest, while their leaders contemplated whether they ought to advance on Shrewsbury. It seems likely that at this point they received word that the North and South Shropshire Yeomanry Cavalry were heading their way under the Hon. Thomas Kenyon, along with about 100 special constables, scores of policemen, an artillery battery and even a contingent of Chelsea pensioners! Although details of the following events are sketchy, it seems that a group of about 200-300 colliers decided to confront this force at Chirk Bridge, and when the two sides met there was 'a scuffle even more dangerous' than that at Gutter Hill. Fighting broke out in what has been called popularly 'the last battle on British soil', and many injuries were inflicted on both sides, especially when three of the strikers' leaders were arrested. The Riot Act was read once more, but before the soldiers' cannon could open fire the miners dispersed and the 'Battle of the Border (or Chirk Bridge)' was over.

The confrontation at Chirk Bridge put an end to 'the last labourers' revolt' in north-east Wales, but the upper orders remained extremely unnerved by the recent turn of events for some time. Indeed, on 5 January 1831, one of numerous 'alarums' brought out hundreds of special constables and others armed with 'flails, fire-tongs, warming pans and truncheons' in the Overton area, and they helped cavalry units to 'defend' the bridges there and at Bangor-on-Dee. Although there were rumblings of discontent in the vicinity their presence deterred any would-be rioters from starting any major trouble, and by 6 January things had settled down again.

However, at the end of January 1831, it became clear that the owners of the hated Acrefair truck shop and pits at Hawarden, Brymbo and elsewhere had reneged on their apparent promises to the people, and so there were 'fresh turn-outs at Ffrwd (Brymbo) and Coed Talon' near Mold. The Yeomanry and special constables armed with sabres were called in to crush the riots, and having done so some of their leaders were arrested. Although some of the striking colliers had managed to gain and retain better wages, early in February 1831 the mineowners of Wrexham secured reinforcements from the 53rd Regiment at Chester, and, fortified by this additional manpower, they set about the arrest of the leaders of the 1830 strikes and some of the 'heroes of the crowd'. A number of men appeared before Ruthin magistrates in May 1831, and although they were treated with customary leniency (because of the Justices' fear that any punishments inflicted upon them would set off renewed disturbances), the coal magnates had eliminated much of the union leadership and were well on their way to breaking the fledgling union by the end of the year.[162]

On 2 June 1831, the authorities arrested several more men who had led the riots of that January, and the tension that was building up beneath the surface erupted in July when the mine owners introduced about 50 men from Anglesey into local pits. The mines at Holywell, Brymbo, Mold and elsewhere shut down as the workers went on strike, and the Mold magistrates warned that without the presence of the Flintshire Yeomanry Cavalry in the town at that time there would be turmoil. Sure enough, during the early hours of 6 July, 300 or so colliers led by three trade union representatives gathered outside the Bromfield shaft at Mold, where they were joined by some 200 men from Flint and around 500 from Holywell and other mines. At *4am* they broke into the lodgings of the 'Anglesey pigs' in the town and the newcomers were forced into the street and then frog-marched through the town by a mob armed with sticks and stones who handled them roughly and called them derisory names such as 'knobsticks'! The homes of the mine owners in the Mold area were attacked as well, and one of the pits' Irish agents was driven along with the miners of Ynys Môn by the 1,000-plus local colliers through Northop, Bagillt and Flint, where they were 'ordered ... to return home'. Some time later the Mold magistrates secured the Flintshire Yeomanry to deal with the miners' disturbances, but their shaken managers urged them to gain additional reinforcements from the 53rd Regiment at Chester to protect the town, and shortly afterwards a troop of the 8th Hussars arrived in Mold. Thereafter, a relative calm returned to the district, and although three men were arrested for rioting and tried at Mold, the jury returned a verdict of 'Not guilty' on all counts – like so many others before them – and things settled down again.[163]

During the summer and autumn of 1831, the coal-mine owners and managers stepped up their efforts to eradicate trade unionism from their pits and by November the whole of the Flintshire coalfield had responded with a mass walk-out. Fresh rioting occurred at Mostyn during October and the services of the Flintshire Yeomanry were called upon once more to crush the miners' resistance. Thereafter, the pit owner, John Eyton, succeeded in pressuring the Mostyn colliers to relinquish their union membership and return to work in return for a pay increase. Following this defeat for the coal workers the authorities braced themselves for further trouble, and on 18 November 1831 the cavalry were obliged to send troopers to prevent any disturbance in Holywell, Greenfield, Hawarden and Mold. Although this military demonstration of force' prevented any disorders in Hawarden and Greenfield, rioting was soon underway elsewhere and the Yeomanry had to stay in the county town, Hawarden and in Holywell for between two and four days. Eventually the military got the upper hand and the coalmen were pushed into making a compromise deal similar to that struck at Bagillt, and in the following weeks the rest of the coalfield made similar bargains with their employers and all the men were back at work by December.

This marked the end of the first trade union in Flintshire and Denbighshire, though the miners' militancy was not diminished by their defeat, and they still had the strike and riot weapons at their disposal. Indeed, on 27 December they utilised both at Mold, where the Flintshire Yeomanry again had to stop the colliers from 'causing much disturbance there'. And there was more 'trouble' with the miners in the New Year, including further disturbances at Rhos, and within a year or two the authorities in Mold had learned their lesson and established a permanent barracks in the town.[164]

Chartism, Rebecca and more local issues 1834-44

By 1837 a new working class movement called 'Chartism' was spreading across Britain, and within its ideological umbrella it incorporated a variety of popular demands on the Establishment, ranging from the fundamental political right of 'one man, one vote', to better pay, working practices and conditions – notably a maximum working day of ten hours , improved food and lower prices, rent and tithe reform, and the dissolution of the workhouse system created under the terms of the Poor Law Ammendment Act of 1834.[165] Some historians assert that there were no Chartist activists in north-east Wales, but there was considerable Chartist sentiment in the region,[166] in which the movement was said to be 'very strong'. Some prominent gentlemen in the Wrexham area such as Richard Bowen of Cefn Mawr were confirmed supporters of Chartism, and although the pacifying influence of the Methodists may well have dissuaded the population as a whole from participating in the nationwide Chartist rioting of 1842 (as it did in Cornwall), industrial labourers in Wrexham and Ruabon did take up the Chartist torch, and around 1839, 'soon after ... the (new) Union workhouse' was opened in Wrexham, the colliers of Brymbo and Cefn Mawr were joined by people from around the area in a march on the institution. There the riotous assembly threatened to storm the 'Bastille' ,[167] and this was at least one clear manifestation of Chartist sentiment in the region.

At the start of the 1840s there were more instances of 'riotous behaviour' by the miners of Hafod colliery at Ruabon, and unemployed colliers from Mold and Chirk roamed the countryside in search of work and food and unsettled many of the places that they visited. Indeed, George Lerry has argued that these men protested about the lack of food available to them and their families 'in much stronger terms' than their ancestors had done a hundred years before, in 1740, though they do not appear to have created any disturbances on the scale of the 18th century corn riots or inflicted any fatalities.[168] Nonetheless, in many districts where Methodism had not yet taken a grip of the people, riots still broke out when the locals felt extremely aggrieved about something, and at Hawarden in April 1842 the employment of a new mine agent by the name of Stanley led to a violent confrontation between the management and the workforce. Many of the Hawarden colliers asserted that Mr Stanley had introduced cheap labour into the Bagillt pits in 1819 and caused their comrades to riot there. Fearing that he would try to do the same in Hawarden hundreds of miners left the pit-heads and broke into his office. They dragged him outside and then amidst scenes of great 'tumult' forced him to march all the way to the railway station at Queensferry, where he was put on a train and, in time honoured fashion, told never to return to Wales. Not long after, however, the miners got word that Stanley had returned to the area and was ensconced in the proprietor's house. Soon this was surrounded by 300 incensed coalmen, and Mr L Rigby, the mine owner, nervously emerged to tell the mob that Stanley had already run off and would not be back again. The colliers left their employer unconvinced of Stanley's sincerity and rallied support at neighbouring pits, whose labour joined them on strike. But after three weeks neither hide nor hair of the despised Stanley had been seen in the district, and the satisfied miners at last returned to work.[169]

By 1843, the influence of 'Rebecca's Daughters' was also spreading from the movement's power-base in south and mid-Wales to the north-east of the country. The Rebecca rioters, like the Chartists, were motivated by a host of grievances, such as poverty, the New Poor Law, food shortages, English absentee landlords, rents, and tithes,[170] but the spark that lit the powder keg was the introduction of high toll charges by turn-pike trusts for the use of their roads. This hit small farmers and tradesmen particularly badly, and drawing inspiration from the Biblical Rebecca to oppose the toll-gates, groups of men dressed in women's clothes decided to pull them down and riot. While most historians have ignored the influence of Rebeccaism in north-east Wales, as they have Chartism, there were at least some of her 'Daughters' active in Flintshire and Denbighshire, and during the autumn of 1843 over '30 farm out-buildings and ricks (were) ... set on fire in Denbighshire' and even more in Flintshire by activists protesting about 'tithes and rents'. Furthermore, on 21 November 1843 the Mardy (now Maerdy) Toll Gate on the Holyhead road not far from Corwen 'was entirely taken away' by a mob of Rebeccaites. Presumably dressed up as women, they sawed down the wooden gate posts and violently demolished the gate house, leaving behind only a note revealing that the destruction was the handiwork of 'Sister Rebecca, with a caution against placing another in (the) ... neighbourhood'. Finally, the influence of Rebecca was strong in the area around Meliden during 1844, and about this time large gatherings at the monthly fair frequently degenerated into mass brawls and riots.[171]

The Flintshire colliers were also restive at the start of 1844, and during January and February miners went out on strike and rioted in Mold, Northop and Hawarden. The disturbances soon spread to the Holywell area and on 1 February a mob of 200 colliers 'surrounded the yards ... of the (Dingle and Englefield) collieries of Messrs (Henry) Crockford and (Samuel Savage) Kenrick' in Greenfield and Holywell. The miners caused significant ructions and prevented the works operating, and the magistrates responded by sending in the Yeomanry against them. In addition they acquired reinforcements from Chester, and within a short space of time the mob leaders were arrested and incarcerated. This brought out other pits in the county in a protest that lasted until March 1844, but eventually the Flintshire colliers simmered down and they all went back to work.[172]

Industrial, political and other disputes, 1850-68

The coal miners of Ffrwd near Brymbo were involved in another bout of large scale violence during March 1850 which was the culmination of a disagreement about leasing arrangements at the Coed-y-brain pit. A Mr Thomas Clayton had purchased the shaft in January 1849 and subsequently leased it to a Mr Thompson. Early in 1850, the lessor declared his intent to repossess the mine in the near future, but the lease-holder asserted that the contract had not yet expired and so he had no right to do so. Expecting to meet resistance when he attempted to retake the works, Clayton set out 'in the dead of night' on 4 March with about 70 men accompanying him. Mr Edward Watkin, the manager of the pit for Mr Thompson, learned of the raiding party and gathered about a dozen miners, some of them armed with sticks, at the machine rooms before Clayton *et al* arrived at around 1am. When he and a dozen of his Lancashire miners entered the buildings carrying tools, such as axes and hammers, with the intent of removing the whimsey and other vital mining equipment, Thompson's men barred their way. Although both sides subsequently blamed each other for the trouble that followed, it appears that a scuffle started in which a Mr Ellison, one of the Clayton men, accidentally or otherwise struck 'one old man with a chisel' and things then escalated. Ellison was set upon by three or four men who called him 'a damned Lancashire (Master's) doggie' and, as one witness testified, he staggered to 'one lot of people ... (who) hammered him and he shouted 'Oh!' (and then) he ran to another lot and they hammered him!' In the melee one of Clayton's men, Mr T Fisher, reportedly 'stepped forward with very insulting language' and a large stone in his hands, and he 'swore he'd kill Watkin ... on the spot'. The mine manager apparently retorted '(you'll) all be killed if you don't go off', or words to that effect, and at this point the Lancashire raiders retreated.

Following their unsuccessful bid to put Thompson's enterprise out of action, Mr Ellison sent for the Wrexham police to intervene on their behalf, and at about five o'clock that morning two policemen arrived at the mine. By this time the machine rooms had been reinforced by about 70 of Mr Thompson's colliers, and after some discussion the two officers decided to confront them, with Mr Clayton's men backing them up. At around 6am they approached the pit-heads, and Constable J O'Donnell recalled later that one of the miners inside the housing, a Mr D Williams, declared that he would protect the gear within to 'the last drop of his blood'. Thomas Clayton was not perturbed by this threat, however, and simply said 'go to work lads', which resulted in 'a complete riot'. Mr Ellison testified that when he got within about 50 yards of the buildings he was fired at with a gun, and Clayton, who was carrying 'a brace of pistols with him', handed over one to PC O'Donnell upon his request. During the riot 'all the men were fighting' and there was much 'hallowing and shouting and making (of) ... attacks', one of which was directed at Clayton's book-keeper, Mr F Hutchison, by a man named W Williams, who reportedly cried 'Damn him! Kill him!'. Another of Thompson's employees made a counter accusation that the Constable pointed his pistol at him and threatened to 'blow your brains out' during the rioting, but Constable O'Donnell argued 'I then considered my life in danger as well as (that of) Hutchison'. In the event it seems that the policemen did not resort to opening fire on the rabble, and eventually 'the Police stopped the' two factions from fighting and then organised a hasty retreat of Clayton's mob, taking with them two of the rioters. The defendants were charged with 'Riot and Assault' and tried at Ruthin on 1 April 1850, and while the Grand Jury agreed that the accused had used more than the 'reasonable force' that was allowed in law to protect Mr Thompson's property and rights, they acquitted them anyway! The magistrates expressed their fears that this would provide a green-light for troublemakers and would undermine the 'peace of the neighbourhood'[173] and it was not long before these were realised.

In 1850, the colliers of Holywell withdrew their labour when two Cornish agents were employed at their pits, and they were soon joined on strike by their colleagues in Halkyn, along with the lead miners of Talargoch. About 500 men armed with sticks marched on the Holywell mines and in scenes of familiar chaos forcibly ousted the 'foreigners' from the area and so forestalled the introduction of a new shift system that most of the region's miners consistently and bitterly opposed.[174] There was a similar rumpus at Treuddyn near Mold, when a mine manager was violently ejected from his premises,[175] and yet more violence by miners at their workplaces in Holywell and Meliden accompanied their strike of 1852.[176]

Between 1852 and 1854 Denbigh was wracked by numerous disturbances as well, but in this case the reason for public disquiet and violence were the payments, known as the church rate, demanded of non-conformists by an increasingly alien established Anglican Church. In a forerunner of the much greater troubles that would strike north Wales almost 35 years later, the church authorities were obliged to try to force non-payers of the rate to meet their customary obligation by sending in bailiffs to distrain their property or other assets, which then could be sold off by auction. Small scale rioting often flared up when such distraint sales were attempted, and in addition to breaking furniture and assaulting bailiffs, one incident involved a major struggle over the attempted removal from the house of the non-conformist leader, Mr Thomas Gee, of a giant 60lb cheese! [177]

More serious ructions attended the colliers' strikes of 1856, when miners in the Wrexham area protested against new working conditions and a cut in their pay. At a mass meeting held on 1 August in the age-old rallying spot of Rhos, large crowds were whipped up by speakers including several of the leaders of the 1830-31 Christmas riots in the district, such as the prize fighter John Jarvis. After lighting bonfires in the village the mob proceeded to Acrefair, where Jarvis picked upon the current representative of his old adversary, the British Iron Company. The colliers and their backers surrounded the home of the Acrefair Works' new Northumbrian agent, Mr Hynde, and when he could not be found 'the mob burst into the house, smashed the furniture' and ransacked the place. Thereafter the rioters made a considerable commotion in the locality, and on 2 August the local magistrate felt it necessary to bring in 140 troops from Wrexham to ensure that no more rioting occurred.[178]

At this time too the lead miners of Talargoch were striking over reductions in their pay, and during July they had blocked the entrances to their works to prevent the management introducing blackleg labour from outside the district. Indeed, any miner who failed to turn up at the picket lines each day was stripped of his trousers and forced to run half-naked through the village! By the end of the month the strikers' frustrations boiled over into violence and enclosure fences on former common lands near the mines were torn down at neighbouring Tywyn.

Then, on 1 August 1856, the same day as the attack directed at the mine manager in Acrefair, the Talargoch mine agent was the victim of a raid on his home at Dyserth Hall. It is quite possible that these incidents were coordinated by the two groups of strikers, for labourers often passed on news as they travelled between the mining communities, and this would have added to the impact of each. The Talargoch men additionally decided to try to unnerve their boss by being 'dressed in women's clothes' in the manner of the Rebeccaites, who had been active in the vicinity a decade or so before. Up to 30 skirt-clad men with 'fire-arms' surrounded the Hall during the evening and 'several shots ... (were) fired' at it, though no casualties were inflicted. In spite of this assault on his home, attempts to sabotage the mine's pumping engines, and several threatening letters, the mine manager refused to make any concessions to the strikers, who in consequence refused to return to work throughout the summer months. Eventually, the mine owner's patience ran out, and on 21October he shipped in a group of strike-breakers to resume work at the face. That night, a band of more than 30 of the self proclaimed 'Meliden Militia ... some armed', laid siege to their lead mine at Talargoch. They demolished several walls, fired at the engine house, wounding in the legs the night-watchman, Edward Thomas, and caused a major disturbance during the night. On the following morning the local Magistrate requested and received a platoon of soldiers (36 men) from Chester, and they guarded the mine and patrolled the area for one week. A huge reward of £200 was offered by the pit proprietor for information on 'the rioters', and after a series of arrests were made the rest of the miners reluctantly returned to work under unwelcome new working conditions.[179]

The final recorded disorders of the 1850s predictably involved colliers, this time at Ruabon, where the men had been striking in 1859 after a slump in the coal trade resulted in a wage cut by the management. One of the pickets, James Davies, was arrested for intimidating men who wanted to return to work, and when news of this got back to the miners about 600 of them 'armed with pick-shafts, posted themselves on Ruabon bridge', determined to stop the police from imprisoning him. Urged on by their vociferously vocal womenfolk, they set up road blocks and did all manner of nuisance in the area, but the police learned of their plans and took their carriage by another route, thereby avoiding a major confrontation.[180]

Another rather dramatic miners' riot was staged near Mold during 1863. About 600 colliers from the Coed Talon Coal Company's pits filed out of them when six of their colleagues were sacked by the Manager, named in different accounts as Dougan or Gregson, who replaced them with men from Lancashire. Anti-English sentiments in the district were fanned by this precipitate action and soon some 2,000 people had assembled ready to march in protest to the mine owner's home at Leeswood. There the colliers' spokesmen demanded the reinstatement of their work-mates, but despite the threats of the mob they received no ground. The precise course of the events that followed are not clear, but it seems that some of the miners' wives accosted the mine manager, and amidst some furious jostling several shots were fired and a miner was wounded. This set off rioting in which a number of houses were battered and stoned in the locality, and the mob seized the new English workers from Coed Talon and then drove them, along with Mr Dougan, towards the railway station at Mold. On entering the town the manager somehow managed to escape from the mob and hid behind flour sacks in a grocer's shop, but the other men were unceremoniously bundled onto a train and, like so many strangers who had tried to work in the area before them, they were told in no uncertain terms that there would not be a welcome in the hillsides of this part of Wales if they ever returned! The miners claimed another victory over industrial tyranny, and although 16 of them were summonsed for 'rioting' a short time after, all of those tried at Mold were characteristically acquitted by a jury of their peers.[181]

A similar disturbance in which a coal mine's manager was forcibly removed by his employees and packed onto a train occurred at Mostyn in 1864,[182] and at this juncture the newly formed Flintshire Constabulary (founded in 1856), also had to contend with numerous 'disorderly ... inhabitants (of the main towns, especially Mold and Holywell), and the vandalism of 'parties of young men'. Additionally, there were spates of incendiary attacks against properties across Flintshire and Denbighshire during 1863-64, for which 80 people were eventually charged (most of them vagrants), and in March 1865 Denbighshire suffered a particularly intense arson campaign. [183]

At the end of 1865, John Taylor, the Cornish mine engineer, returned to Halkyn some 33 years after he had provoked riots by its colliers when he had attempted to bring in a new 'improved' system of working hours there. Despite the length of time that had elapsed, memories in the mining community were long, and when he made a renewed effort to introduce a new pattern of Cornish eight-hour shifts in December 1865 nearly all of the 50 colliers at the Pant-y-gof pit went on strike. The picket stayed on duty throughout the Christmas period, and then on 11 January 1866 rumours abounded that blackleg labour was to be brought in by the management. 'Several hundred miners (from nearby shafts) marched in procession to Pant-y-Gof' to demonstrate their solidarity and to blockade the mine entrance, and they remained on call for a number of days. Then, on 16 January, with about 2,000 miners congregated in the area from all over Holywell and district, violence broke out and a few local cottages were ransacked. Mr Taylor and his associates pressed the local magistrate to prevent any further rioting, and on 18 January a Company of the 85th Regiment from Chester were billeted at nearby Holywell. By this time the mass pickets had disappeared from the scene back to their own pits, and fortified by the presence of the soldiers, Mr Taylor and the magistrate addressed the remaining Halkyn pickets, who numbered about 100 men, and informed them that the military would escort those who wanted to work into the mine on the following day and that no trouble would be tolerated. On 19 January a number of policemen, supported by the army who were held in reserve, escorted five strike-breakers into the works yard without incident, and this set a pattern for the next couple of months. In March, the troops left the area and on 1May a mob of up to 1,000 miners gathered to bar the way to some 20 working miners. When they tried to enter their pit some of them were seized by the crowd and their lodgings were targeted for destruction. Eight of the kidnapped men 'were roughly handled' and force-marched through the country lanes to Holywell, thence to Greenfield and the port of Mostyn. Evidently the strikers planned to literally ship them out of the county, but at the dockside three police constables confronted the mob and secured the release of the men. In the light of this bother, police reinforcements were brought in to watch over the pickets at Halkyn aboard two omnibuses from Holywell and Chester, and they included the Chief Constable of Flintshire. He decided that action must be taken to put an end to the disturbances, and at 2am on 28 May squads of police, some of them armed with cutlasses, broke down the doors of the suspected ring-leaders' homes and dragged the men dazed and confused from their beds and into custody. They were charged for their part in the rioting on 11 June, at Mold, and a mob of between 2,000 and 3,000 who had gathered outside the old court-house were held back by policemen and soldiers from Flintshire and a detachment of the 39th Regiment from Chester. At the hearing the 14 men were committed for trial at Chester in April 1867, and the rest of the day seems to have passed off without any further popular protests in Mold. The strike continued in spite of this set-back but on 14

December 1866 the men returned to Pant-y-gof on the manager's terms. Notwithstanding their defeat, the Halkyn miners organised another stoppage during March 1867, and with several hundred supporters caused a sizable disturbance, for which, in this case, nobody was charged. On 5 April though, four of the Halkyn strike leaders were sentenced to terms of hard labour for fomenting trouble and rioting,[184] and this somewhat unusual success for the Establishment during a period of relative political calm greatly rankled the Flintshire mining community and would not be forgotten.

In March 1868 it was the turn of the Ruabon colliers to take strike action when a 10% wage cut was imposed upon them. Near their own pits and in Wrexham, where 'the old Chartist political traditions were by no means dead', the miners and their large number of followers engaged in unbridled disorder. This included the forcible ejection of pit managers from both towns, and a bailiff by the name of Johnson was apparently pursued a distance by 400 riotous miners and had to seek shelter at Wynnstay Hall.[185]

The last riots of the 1860s, not surprisingly involved colliers and those of 1869 at Leeswood and Mold received not only national publicity, they were even reported to the Communist International by none other than Karl Marx!

Industrial, political and other disputes, 1869-86

On 1 May 1869, John Young, the Northumbrian manager of the Leeswood Green colliery, near Mold, announced to his workers that as from 17 May their wages would be cut (and in any case the Welsh miners were paid only half the rate of the Englishmen working at the colliery). The new wage policy was duly implemented, and on 19 May at least 60 miners, led by one Ishmael Jones, converged on their manager's house and 'old Young's Troubles' began. As more and more people collected at the spot where the miners were challenging Mr Young to face them, 'the growing crowd became violent ... and it was decided to send him packing ... (following the) traditional miners' practice'. He was pulled out of his dwelling and then paraded through Pontybodkin and Pontblyddyn, but at Hope Junction station two police constables intervened and rescued the Manager from the mob and then took him for protection to Mold police station. This raised the temperature in the district, and on 21 May 'there was a further colliery riot in Leeswood' during which Young's home was ransacked and his furniture carried to the railway station at Mold ready for his departure! A Coed Talon collier, William Hughes, was then arrested for his part in the original attack on John Young, and locked up in the cells at Mold police station. On 25 May, as Hughes was being escorted by four policemen to a hearing at the adjacent court-house, they were opposed by a rout of up to 1500 people, including colliers from Treuddyn, Leeswood, Nercwys, Broncoed, Mold and Buckley. Many of them wielded 'oak sticks, pick handles and truncheons of the most formidable nature', as one reporter put it, and they had come out both because of a wish to support their brother miner, and to express their nationalistic feelings against overbearing English masters. As the colliers charged into the police, flailing their batons, many shouted

'A Country is stronger than its Lord!', and having secured the release of their comrade and the flight of the police officers they carried Hughes shoulder-high through King Street and Wrexham Street, to ecstatic cheers from the hoi polloi. Later that day, however, the hero of the hour decided that it may be the most sensible course of action to give himself up to the authorities, and soon afterwards he appeared before a magistrate and was bailed to return for trial on 2 June. In addition, warrants for seven other suspected rioters were issued, and it was not long before all were in custody at Mold, apparently having given themselves up at the behest of a Methodist mine leader, David Phillips, who believed that their aims would be best served by non-violent forms of protest rather than by rioting.

As the news of the eight colliers' incarceration spread there was uproar at many local pits, notably in Brymbo, and when the men were due to be tried at Mold, on 2 June, about 600 coalmen joined the ever growing multitude outside the court house at around 11*am*. By the afternoon there were in the region of 2,000 persons milling about the Hall Fields in Mold, where they were addressed by David Phillips and other Methodists who preached forbearance and restraint. There was in fact quite a convivial atmosphere at the time, with many family groups enjoying a day out, and only a 'few lads (hanging about brandishing) ... cudgels or sticks' near the court building on Chester Street. At 5 o'clock, however, the presiding judge handed out heavy fines on six of the defendants including Will Hughes, and Ishmael and John Jones were consigned to one month's hard labour.

The crowd were angered by these sentences and utterly incensed when they learned of the judge's anti-Welsh summary of the case, and, with their nationalist sentiments aroused, trouble broke out when the Joneses emerged from the court-house at 7*pm*. They were escorted by 39 Flintshire policemen and 56 soldiers who had been drafted in from Chester in anticipation of violence, and it seems that the men of the 2nd Battalion, the 4th (King's Own) Regiment became the focus of the canaille's nationalistic fury. Three groups of some 500 people each converged on the prison party, led by 'sturdy collier youths (and) ... almost immediately' some of the women started to throw stones at the soldiers. There were plenty of projectiles readily to hand on a building site adjacent to Tyddyn Street, and before the security forces and their prisoners had made much progress towards the waiting train at the railway station, approximately 200 yards away, a rain of rocks, many 4-5lbs in weight, fell upon them. A journalist wrote that a five year old boy stood stranded by a nearby wall and 'cowered down as the stones rattled ... about him'. The deluge of thousands of stones went on for 'at least ten minutes', not only against the soldiers and police but also the railway engine and carriages, the station telegraph office, and the platforms. The windows of the rail express and the station canopies were shattered and furniture destroyed, but the police and soldiers eventually made it to the station buildings, and at least one PC tried to hurl back some of the missiles that were falling down 'mercilessly ... (and) as thick as hail'. As a result of this prolonged bombardment no less than 23 troopers and 13 policemen were frightful(ly) injured (and) ... bleeding copiously' from head and other wounds, and every single man received some degree of trauma. One of the most seriously hurt, the platoon commanding officer, Captain Blake, was implored to give the order to open fire by the Chief Constable of Flintshire, Peter Browne, who believed that if he did not they would all be killed. But in spite of the fact that 'several of the policemen showed their helmets (to be) completely cut in two by the stones', and mistaken reports that one of the Privates had been mortally wounded by the mob, the

Captain showed great restraint and refused to order his men to open fire unless they were authorised to do so by a magistrate. Chief Constable Browne then raced down the platform to the train and bundled a Chester JP, Mr Clough, out into the melee, where he very quickly gave permission for the Riot Act to be read and the soldiers made ready to shoot.

Under the incessant barrage at the station, a normal reading of the Riot Act proved 'utterly impossible', and as the frenzied crowd 'stormed the railway platform' some of the battered soldiers fired blank shots over the heads of those leading the assault. This had no effect on them though, and so at last Captain Blake authorised his men to use live ammunition against the masses 'at intervals' in controlled firing. Up to fifteen shots were discharged before the commanding officer ordered a halt and, as a result of the shooting, two colliers and a woman who had been throwing sticks and stones were shot dead, along with another woman who was said to have been a 'spectator'. One of the fatalities, Robert Hannaby, was struck by a bullet that 'caught him on the cheek bone, entering the head and causing the brain to protrude', killing him instantly. The others shot by the soldiers died of their wounds some time later. In addition, a male 'passer-by' was grievously wounded by gun-fire, a man lost several fingers from one round, and a little girl one of her ears. Evidently they were the casualties of fire from frightened, angered and panicky young troopers, and it was perhaps fortunate that their commanding officer acted so calmly or the tragedy that occurred could have been even worse. As it was, once the military had forced the rabble into retreat they were able to arrest five men and then board the train with their prisoners and depart, while the people tended to their dead and wounded and eventually began to disperse from the scene at about 9pm.

On receiving news of the lethal Mold riot, the authorities despatched to the town a full company of soldiers from Chester. They were housed at the Market Hall and *Black Lion Inn* until 10 June, by which time relative normality had been restored to the neighbourhood. However, when the despised Mr Young returned to Mold on 22 July he was abducted once more by a group of colliers and their wives, led by the embittered David Phillips, and he was obliged to walk passed jeering spectators through Pontblyddyn and Buckley to Queensferry. There he was ordered to take the train out of the country and never to darken it again. Thereafter, on 6 August 1869, Phillips the orator and two other men were tried for their part in this affair, along with ten men who were charged with rioting on 2 June at Mold. Phillips and his fellow accused got between 3 and 18 months of hard labour, while half of those on trial for the Mold riot were found guilty and sentenced to ten years in prison. The historian D J V Jones has noted that from the 1860s onwards fewer people were being arrested and convicted for rioting in Wales than in previous decades,[186] but the trend appears to have been the reverse in the north-east of the country. Indeed, the severe sentences and the loss of the four 'Mold Martyrs' seem to have subdued the miners of the area once and for all, and they took no further part in colliery riots in the area.

While working class resistance was quiesced in Mold by the 1870s, other places remained notorious for their street violence, particularly Wrexham, where its miners continued to make

Facing: The Mold Riot of 2 June 1869. This print, showing the beleaguered troops and police defending themselves at the railway station, was produced by the Mold firm of Pring & Price and was probably the basis of the picture which appeared in the Illustrated London News.

their feelings felt through violent means when they deemed it necessary to use them. During October 1875 the colliers of Brymbo, Coedpoeth, Cefn and Rhos struck over changes in their conditions, and 'intimidation on a large scale was carried on. Bands of 60 strikers at most of the pits in Brymbo' stopped men entering them and despite the presence of numbers of police, sporadic disturbances went on until the miners returned to work en-masse in mid-December 1875.[187]

Rhos was also the site of more industrial turmoil at the Bromfield pit in 1878, when magistrates felt obliged to call in a detachment of soldiers from the Wrexham Barracks to 'aid the civil authorities in quelling a riot'. The Rhos miners additionally rioted at the Hafod pit at the end of the decade, and a mine manager's 'house was sacked and almost demolished' in customary fashion.[188]

The Rhos men, and thousands of their colleagues from numerous pits in the Wrexham and Ruabon areas, walked out in March 1882 over another imposed pay cut, and on 19 April several hundred of them blocked their premises and caused major disturbances in Ruabon when they set about destroying some of the industrial plant there. The authorities were prepared for the rioters, however, and 'a strong detachment of the Royal Welch Fusiliers (3rd [Militia] Battalion), armed with bayonets, rifles and ball cartridges' went into action, badly injuring several of the colliers and swiftly ending the rioting. The Officer Commanding,, Lt Colonel Sir Robert Cunliffe, next stationed police constables and specials, accompanied by two companies of soldiers, on various strategic roads and at other vulnerable points so as to prevent miners from Rhos, Pen-y-cae, Ruabon and Acrefair heading for numerous pit owners' homes and attacking them. The 'presence of the troops prevented any further rioting' in the locale, and while it lasted it must have been particularly severe because the Chief Constable of Denbighshire, Major Leadbetter, decided that in the circumstances he should allow the issue of cutlasses to his men, under rules laid down by the Secretary of State in 1857 that afforded their use for the personal protection of policemen when magistrates believed that 'rioting is serious'. In a General Order of 24 April 1882 Major Leadbetter stated that cutlasses were being made available 'in consequence of the disturbed state of the district and rumours of intended Riot'. But he warned that swords must be used 'only in extreme cases of self-defence when (officers feel that they are) in actual danger of (losing) life or limb, or in conjunction with the military power they are charging the Mob after the Riot Act has been read (and) even then the Chief Constable hopes (that) no man will be carried away by excitement and will only use his weapon when necessity requires'. In spite of the availability of this unusual piece of anti-riot equipment, when 'serious rioting' restarted at the Westminster colliery in the Moss and Cerney area, not far from Brymbo, the police apparently had not been provided with any specialist kit, and undoubtedly this would have jeopardised their safety. As blackleg labour was brought into the Westminster pit hundreds of colliers hurled stones at them and their police guard, and reportedly the heavily outnumbered constables were chased by the miners all the way to Wrexham! The Deputy Chief Constable of Denbighshire returned to the colliery with 14 officers, determined to take the strike-breakers into the works, but again the police were 'met with a shower of stones' and had to beat a hasty retreat, with the pit manager, into out-buildings, where they somewhat foolhardily captured one of the strikers'. This led to an intense bombardment with large rocks, and 'crowds from the hill behind the offices rolled down big stones upon the roof'. When all the windows had been smashed and the building all but flattened the police at last freed their captive in the hope that the rioters would cease their offensive. But the barrage of boulders and other objects by the enraged miners continued unabated, and so the policemen decided to make a mad dash 'for it, and they fought their way through the crowd with fist and baton'. When they arrived back at Wrexham police station, all of them had to be treated for serious injuries, and they probably had been lucky to escape with their lives. Those in power then sanctioned the use of the Royal Welch Fusiliers and several companies of the Militia, who arrived at the Westminster mine 'with fixed bayonets and had the Riot Act read by a magistrate', which produced the desired effect of clearing the rioters from the streets.

Although the colliers undertook peaceful picketing for some weeks after the trouble at Moss, 'threatening bands of colliers' from there joined forces with men from Rhos and the Southsea colliery near Coedpoeth, to barrack some of its miners who were continuing to work. By June they had to be escorted through ranks of vociferous strikers by police and soldiers, and for a good few days large numbers of colliers turned up at Coedpoeth, 'each carrying his cudgel (and intending) to attack and vandalise as much as possible'. The presence of the army and 'many chapel deacons' prevented any major disorders though, and by the middle of June 1882 all the miners had returned to work and the unrest soon dissipated.[189]

Another management attempt to cut miners' pay during a slump in coal prices resulted in a lock-out at Buckley on 26 August 1884, and 600 men took part in mass pickets for several months after that. By 24 November though, some 20 colliers had decided to return to work, led by a native of Cheshire, and at the Maes-y-grug pit 'there were rumours of a riot in the air'. Over 100 miners rushed from Sychdyn and New Brighton to the pit-head and there 'a demonstration of hostility towards the blacklegs' was organised, but a large police presence enabled them to enter the premises. 'Threats and intimidation continued throughout the winter', however, and in January 1885 there was another confrontation between the police and the striking miners that flared up into trouble. But, they did not prevent the returnees from working, and by the end of the month all the colliers had joined them back at work.[190]

In the winter of 1885-86 tension was rising all across Denbighshire and Flintshire because of the impending general election, in which more men would be voting than ever before, and which therefore offered more opportunities for rival factions to clash with each other over policies and personalities. On 13 November 1885, Major Leadbetter, the Chief Constable of Denbighshire, issued a General Order outlining how the Force should police the large political meetings expected in the county and deal with any ferment or riots arising at them. He urged his officers not to intervene 'if at all possible', but if the principle of 'non-interference' (designed to avoid any accusations of the police provoking trouble) could not be adhered to because of the circumstances prevailing in any given situation, then his men were instructed to do the 'utmost in their power' to quell any disorders by 'every means' available to them before resorting to the use of physical force. Major Leadbetter clearly wished to avoid any riots at this politically sensitive time, but on 1 December 1885, at the National Schools in Brymbo, there was what one observer dubbed 'one of the most diabolical and disgraceful riots ever witnessed in Wales'. Sir Watkin Williams Wynn, following in his ancestors' footsteps, was offering himself as a prospective candidate for parliament and he was due to speak to his supporters who had rallied inside the school buildings that evening. However, an 'immense crowd of roughs' who loudly expressed their opposing opinions outside became unhinged when Sir Watkin greeted his friends within, and they stoned all the windows of the hall and tried to rush the entrances crying 'Kill him!'. Police and private guards stopped the mob breaking into the hall, but Sir Watkin had to be escorted out to his carriage, and as it sped away it was assailed by the mob with sticks, stones and even an 18-inch long iron bar that burst through the wooden frame and narrowly missed Sir Watkin. Following this 'diabolical outrage at Brymbo' the somewhat ruffled MP-to-be called off scheduled meetings at the nearby Westminster and Southsea collieries, where his supporters feared that further troubles may well accompany any appearance by him.[191]

Only a week later, on 8 December 1885, Irishmen working at the nearby Plas Power colliery 'were mobbed and driven away by (the volatile) Welsh colliers' and told never to return to Brymbo. There was also more strife there on 30 September 1886 when striking Wrexham and Ruabon miners homed in on some of the working miners of Brymbo and 'great damage was done at Plas Power by ... (the) rioters'.[192] Therefore, rioting was still an instrument of protest that the people of north-east Wales were quite accustomed to in the mid-1880s, and during the last years of that decade there were more riots in the region than at any time for more than half a century.

The Tithe War of 1886-91

Over a period of five years a whole series of disturbances broke out across north and mid-Wales as part of a mass popular political movement protesting against the full payment, during a time of recession, of tithes which were a biblically-based 'obligatory donation' to Church funds by farmers, amounting to one-tenth of their income. The tithe troubles were not 'geographically confined to the Vale of Clwyd and Hiraethog areas' of Denbighshire as one popular history asserts, although many of them occurred there. There were also outbreaks elsewhere in that county, as well as in others such as Flintshire and Merionethshire. The scale of the disorders led both contemporaries and some historians to compare the 'Tithe War' to the 'Rebecca Riots', and in fact these had 'created a myth which lived long in the consciousness' of the Welsh population that rioting could bring about political changes. Indeed, many of the tithe rioters 'received fine lessons in direct action (from their forbears and often acted) ... in the manner of the Rebeccaites'.[193] And like the rioters of the 1840s who channelled their anger over numerous issues into the destruction of toll gates, those of 50 odd years later also harboured many deep-seated grievances but focussed on the key issue, the 'tithe rent-charge', by refusing to meet the financial demands of the Church authorities in full or even at all, thereby forcing a distraint sale. Many hundreds of these sales were held and used by the movement's leaders as the focus for non-violent popular protests, but occasionally these became violent flash-points for civil dissension which was either spontaneous or organised by local anti-tithe agitators.

The relationship between much of the population of north-east Wales and the established Church had deteriorated over the course of the 19th century as more and more people shifted from Anglicanism to Non-Conformism, and by the 1850s the latter were in the majority. Violent protests over the collection of the Church Tax in Denbigh during that decade had provided a warning of the possible shape of things to come, and popular dissatisfaction with the Church intensified over the course of the 1860s and 1870s as Welsh nationalism flourished, spurred on by a non-conformist Welsh press that championed the language issue. The rift between Welsh tenants and their absentee English landlords also widened after 1875 when recession led to the eviction of many farmers who could not afford to pay either their rents or for the improvements to their farmsteads that their landlords demanded. The stigma of unemployment and the spectre of the workhouse fuelled the animosity towards the Establishment felt by many farmers.

Following the passing of the Irish Land Act of 1881 that secured more rights for Irish tenants, a Denbighshire and Flintshire Farmers' League was founded and it decided to address the biggest bug-bear of its members, namely the payment of what many perceived as an unfair tax to an alien Church at a time when they could least afford it. The charge was worked out by roving Church Commissioners in conjunction with the local parish rector (who was the 'tithe owner' and received the payment as part of his income), and the land-owner, and the formula used to attain it was to calculate 10% of the average price a farmer was expected to gain at market for his produce over a seven year period if his fields had been planted with equal proportions of barley, wheat and oats, and they had produced the theoretical optimum yield. This patently unwieldy, inaccurate and confusing, not to say ridiculous system, meant that during periods of economic depression like the mid-1880s, when crop prices plummeted, many farmers' incomes fell yet they were still expected to pay the sums that had been worked out on the basis of an income that was significantly higher.

As the authorities distrained more and more hard-pressed farmers' possessions, including their crops and livestock, they produced considerable hardship amongst the non-conformist farming communities of the region, whose burgeoning desire for 'political and social influence to match their numerical strength' was reflected in the 1885 election results when their men took advantage of the recent introduction of secret ballots and voted as they desired rather than as their English masters dictated. As a result, 30 out of the 34 Welsh MPs returned by 'the People' were Liberals, many of whom, like David Lloyd George and Tom Ellis, were militant and nationalist in outlook. Their parliamentary speeches fanned the flames of discontent in Wales and, encouraged by the concurrent agricultural protest campaigns of the Scottish and the Irish, when a poor harvest exacerbated the already desperate position of the north-east Wales farmers during the winter of 1885-86, the anti-tithers sprang into action.[194]

Approaching the end of 1885 many landlords in the Vale of Clwyd came under concerted pressure from their tenants to reduce their rents and some of the more receptive ones granted concessions to them. Their fellow agronomists at Llandyrnog and Llanynys then decided in December to try to convince their parish priests to make similar reductions in the tithe charge, of between 5% and 25%, and in the New Year they granted some discounts to them. Other small-holders soon pressed for the same treatment, and at Holywell in January 1886 self-appointed 'land court' tribunals on the Irish model were set up by farmers. The level of the tithe was reduced in most of the parishes where this was demanded, but distraints still occurred in various places, and 'in some cases bailiffs were maltreated' by local people.

The first major disorders did not occur until August 1886 though, when the Rev Evan

Evans of Llanarmon-yn-Iâl, gave notice to his flock that he would not countenance any reduction in their charge and that all payments must be made on time, or, according to the law, after 10 days' notice bailiffs would be sent to distrain and auction any defaulting farmers' property.[195] This raised the hackles of the whole community, members of which steadfastly refused to pay anything to their parson, and when distraint notices were served on them no Welsh auctioneer could be found who was prepared to undertake the sales. Therefore one from Chester was employed, and on 26 August a distraining party set out for Llanarmon, including 60 policemen from as a far away as Wrexham, evidently in expectation of resistance from the locals. This in fact materialised as the auction began at one farm, with the crowd outside it throwing stones at the police, but the Chief Constable considered that this was 'very trifling'. Nonetheless, his presence indicates that the atmosphere at the time must have been highly charged, and he must have become personally involved to ensure that the emotions running high on both sides did not lead to any major bloodshed. D W Howell argues that the very presence of large numbers of police was 'an incitement to mob riots', but the appearance of English enforcers of what was perceived as an unjust and foreign tax were at least as much of a provocation, and undoubtedly they would have been attacked (as on other previous occasions) whether the police were there or not. Indeed, on 3 September 80 policemen failed to deter a mob engaged in 'much yelling and other excitement' from trying to assault the English auctioneer at Hendre Llwyn Yn farm at Llanfair Dyffryn Clwyd, not very far from Llanarmon. He was said to have been verbally and physically 'threatened and would have been maltreated but for the protection of the police'.

Only a week later, 81 police returned to Llanarmon-yn-Iâl for another distraint, and this time an even bigger crowd of 500 people turned out to attempt to prevent the work of the auctioneer. Doubtless they had been encouraged to attend by their non-conformist preachers who played a 'crucial' role in organising anti-tithe opposition in this and other areas, and in addition 'different groups of protestors were aware of each others' activities (by virtue of the fact that nearby mines) were worked not only by (local) people ... but also by workers from other villages and ... towns' in the district who carried word of sales far and wide. Hence, 30 lime-burners and a group of quarrymen armed with sticks and staves from Minera were among those gathered at Llanarmon on 10 September, and when the auctioneer and his accomplices, including the Rev Evans, arrived at one farm they were pelted with rotten eggs and stones. One of the crowd's leaders, a farmer named John Parry, managed to prevail on them to desist and then spoke to the masses, condemning the vicar for his stubbornness, but also begging the mob to abide by constitutional and lawful means of protest and not engage in any more violence. However, 'in an atmosphere of tension and high excitement' the Minera miners clashed with the two bailiffs and one was savagely 'set upon with staves, beaten about the head and left nearly dead'. About 40 people also pursued and stoned a carriage containing the fleeing vicar, and the auctioneer's clerk was chased a distance by the rabble and had to seek refuge in a nearby house. John A Morgan, a journalist and political agent from Mold, said of the people, 'they were more like demons than anything else'. And as a result of their 'demonic' demonstration the Rev Evans was brought to terms by the farmers of his parish and they agreed upon a 15% reduction in the tithe charge. Nobody was arrested for the rioting of that day and the tithe rioters had gained their first victory.[196]

Following the success of the mob at Llanarmon-yn-Iâl, a group of farmers in the locality decided to form an anti-tithe society that could compensate local farmers whose stock or other means of earning their living were taken away from them for sale by representatives of the Church Commissioners. At a packed meeting at the Liberal Club in Ruthin on 7 September they formed a new Farmers' Tithe Defence League that incorporated Thomas Gee's Land Defence League and similar parochial groups. The new Anti-Tithe League was modelled on the Irish Land League both in form and objectives, which were not only to reform the tithe system, but also to create land courts like those formed at Holywell that could calculate fair rents, to secure rights of tenure and to gain reimbursement for farmers who made improvements to their properties without having received any compensation from their landlords; and to be granted low interest rate loans from the Government. The new League's first chairman was John Parry of Llanarmon, and, like all of the organisation's leadership, he espoused, supported, organised and coordinated mass meetings, demonstrations and protests, and began fund-raising for the anti-tithe campaign. He and other leaders like the publisher Thomas Gee also understood the reasons for and sympathised with those who took part in riots, but they did not openly advocate the use of violence, and this occurred at the behest of local people. Nonetheless, men like Thomas Gee helped to stir emotions that transmutated into rioting on several occasions, and he also gave local activists the opportunity to prepare their resistance to the authorities. The non-conformist publisher advertised details of all distraints in his newspaper *Baner ac Amserau Cymru* and in addition it kept people up-to-date with all tithe-related incidents. The organ praised the tithe 'warriors' and declared that those rights granted to the Irish should apply to the Welsh too, and so at the very least the League and its publicity machine made the possibility of rioting more likely. Indeed, although the historian DJ V Jones has noted that from the 1880s there was less rioting, effigy-burning and the like in Wales than before,[197] once again the trend was bucked in north-east Wales, where traditional forms of popular protest came to the fore from the summer of 1886 onwards.

During the first weeks of December 1886 a series of distraints in the Whitford area near Holywell were undertaken by the Church Commissioners' agents with little fuss, but anti-tithe sentiment was particularly strong roundabouts and so when ten bailiffs, who were described as 'London roughs and Chester scum', were brought in to guard confiscated property and stock, the local inhabitants decided to give them 'a hot time of it'. They were 'completely boycotted and c(ould) ... find neither food nor shelter', and at one farmstead, Mynydd Mostyn, a crowd of 200-300 people opposed two of the bailiffs and chased them for several miles through the countryside. Then, in customary fashion, they were forced onto a train bound for Chester, and thereafter the bailiffs 'were all driven away' from the district by angry crowds.

In view of these proceedings, when a sale was organised for 20 December 1886 in the Whitford locale, 80 policemen from both Flintshire and Denbighshire accompanied the auctioneer and his men to Mostyn railway station. Upon their arrival guns were fired to both warn the populace and to unnerve the interlopers, and soon crowds gathered at Pentreffynnon Farm at Tre Mostyn. John Parry was present and spoke to the throng, urging them to 'rise with the farmers and sweep away the bishops and the Church of Wales', which can hardly have served to calm things down. When the distraint party arrived at the farm they were jeered and then the gathering of 1000-2000 started to pelt their targets with the nearest weapon to hand – snowballs! Within minutes the police and their wards looked 'like Father Christmases' and the mob demanded that the auctioneer be taken to the railway station and sent packing. After about ten minutes the police then tried to push back the crowds from the farm buildings to begin the sale procedure, and eggs, stones and other projectiles were thrown into the farm yard at them. Further, the Deputy Chief Constable of Flintshire, James D Bolton, from Mold, stated that some of the crowd made a hole in a nearby frozen horse-pond and 'a rush was made to force myself and the auctioneer ... through it'! The auctioneer, J E Roberts ap Mwrog, of Rhyl, was said to have made 'very violent pantomimic motions with his walking stick' to keep the crowd at bay, and he 'was hit very frequently' with snowballs! Superintendent Hughes of Holywell later described how things took a turn for the worse at this point, as the mob attacked the police with stones, fence posts and five-foot-long sticks and 'some of the constables' helmets were smashed' under this barrage. Indeed, a journalist at the scene reported that in the melee many of the people sustained 'broken foreheads, some ... black eyes ... and others (were) minus (their) hats, or (had) ... mere apologies for that useful article of attire'!

Following this debacle, the police and sales men decided to withdraw and to try to auction some cattle at another farm, Mynydd Mostyn. But by the time that they arrived there the crowds had grown even bigger – estimated at 4,000-5,000 by a *Daily Post* reporter – and they subjected the party to even more snowballing and a surge that broke the police lines. Hence, the authorities made tracks again, followed by the mob, and Superintendent Hughes said that there was more or less a 'continuous fight' for some six hours.

On arrival at a third holding, Fachallt, near Whitford, the police made a charge into the crowd in an attempt to begin the sale procedure, and 'very strange expletives were made use of'. But they had to give up and move on to Waen farm where the Welsh 'traitor' 'ap Mwrog ... was anathematised in no measured terms'! At this final point of conflict the distraining party decided to call it a day and left with the police, to a chorus of jubilant cheers from the tithe rioters. There is no doubt that they used an appreciable level of violence during these protests, but the mob also exercised a degree of self restraint, for when a 'large stone was thrown' at the police by members of the crowd at one of the farms 'a cry of 'Shame!' ' rose up,[198] and so the rioters limited the level of violence that was used to that which they deemed appropriate for achieving their ends, and which would not obviously undermine the support for their cause.

The day after the Mostyn and Whitford disturbances, 21December, the Chief Constable of Denbighshire went along with 60-70 police, two bailiffs and the rest of the distraining group to the Abergele area. At Ty Gwyn farm, near Pensarn, another sizable assemblage greeted the newcomers and 'the atmosphere was decidedly ugly'. Scuffles with the police broke out and although the violence was not on the scale of the previous day's the crowd went one better in one respect and in a 'serious disturbance' they collared the auctioneer, ap Mwrog, and then threw him into a pond![199]

During December 1886 there was ferment also in the neighbouring district of Colwyn Bay, where the Rev W Venables Williams was sent anonymous letters warning that if he did not reduce the tithe charge he and his vicarage would be 'dynamited and blown up!' This was a distinctly modern terrorist threat, and the means and will to carry it out were undoubtedly available in this quarrying area. Indeed, on 31October, the nearby church at Llandrillo-yn-Rhos had been burned out by activists! [200]

As the Anti-Tithe League concentrated its resources on peaceful protests, propaganda and agitation in the political arena during the first months of 1887, it seems that the common people contented themselves with waiting to see if the authorities would respond favourably to their pressure (and that of anti-tithers as far away as the USA). But with little visible progress being made and distraints continuing as before, pent-up feelings gradually intensified, and when the warmer weather returned so did ructions in Flintshire, Denbighshire and parts of Merionethshire. In May 1887, mobs at Rhyl forcibly prevented sales from going ahead, and at Llandrillo and Cynwyd, near Corwen, the locals were 'in uproar' and turned on bailiffs who were trying to work there.[201] And just over the county boundary in Denbighshire, even more serious rioting burst forth at this time.

At Llangwm, near Cerrigydrudion, a group of farmers and the parish priest, Elwyn o Wyrfai, had come to terms on a 'substantial reduction' of the tithe charge, but on 21 May 1887, high-handed church commissioners refused to validate their agreement and their inflexibility led to a recurrence of violence by elements of the Denbighshire farming community and their supporters. At 3*am* on 25 May, 25 policemen arrived at Llangwm, ready to rendezvous with the auctioneer, his assistants and the bailiffs. But they arrived there late, and this gave the villagers a chance to light bonfires around the place and to rally reinforcements to stop them from undertaking their task. When the Commission's officials attempted to hold a sale at Fron Isaf farm there was 'uproar', as about 100 people hurled eggs, stones and sods of earth at them, and although the auctioneer managed successfully to sell some livestock to one of the men accompanying him, the party was unable to remove them from the premises. The crowd blocked the farm gates while a large land-roller was pulled into position to barricade the narrow lane, and Superintendent Vaughan of the Denbigh police was obliged to lead the party away empty-handed. This boosted the spirits of the community, who were enraged by this interference in their affairs, and thereafter lookouts were posted day and night around the locale to warn if any of the distrainers returned. On 27 May Llangwm's sentries spotted a horse-drawn brake approaching the village with a police escort, and the cry of 'Sale! Sale!' soon went up. A throng of 200-300 locals converged on the arranged assembly point of *Ty Nant Inn*, and there several men made speeches and whipped up the crowd, including a makeshift 'cavalry' of farmers on horse-back who were armed with sticks. One of the mob later testified that as the wagonette neared the village Mr Charles V Stephens, the Commissioners' distraining agent, was manhandled and splattered with eggs, and hence that the wagon driver was ordered to drive through the crowd. Apparently his vehicle hurtled towards the village 'at a terrible speed', where it was attacked by 15-20 men, and then sped off for Disgarth. Some of the people blew horns to warn of its approach, in the manner of the Rebecca rioters, while others banged pots, pans and other metal objects to frighten the horses. By the time that the convoy arrived at Arddwyfaen Farm about 500 people had turned out to greet them, and some 100 men tried to block the road to the farm. However, the distraining party were able to force their way through to the property and there they set about holding an auction. Immediately the rowdies started to throw eggs, stones and turfs at the 'enemy' and then engaged them in hand-to-hand combat. Mr George Thorpe, the agent's clerk, afterwards recalled that the mob were 'mad ... like savages' and that during the fist-fighting his 'trousers were destroyed', although by what means is unclear! He and many of his colleagues were undoubtedly in fear for their lives, for along with the police they were chased in the wagonette for about a quarter of a mile by the mob, many of whom used large shepherd's crooks to try to collar their prey. Amidst all this furore the horses bolted and the trap was smashed to pieces in the narrow lane, and with no other means of escape the police and the auctioneer's coterie found themselves at the mercy of the multitude. Several of the church officials had their coats turned inside-out as a mock symbol of their repentance for their wrong-doings against the Llangwm community, and then they were frog-marched with the police by about 700 people along the Corwen road. Many of them carried red and black flags, the former representing their nationalistic will to serve their fatherland, and the latter signifying mourning, with all its disturbing undertones for the unwelcome visitors. Indeed, at Pont-y-Glyn many of the rabble called for the auctioneer to be thrown over a 60 foot high cliff into the river below, and only the good offices of some Anti-Tithe League leaders (like Thomas Gee's son, Howell) 'stood between the officials and threatened death'. They begged for common sense to prevail, and when the auctioneer and his companions pleaded for their lives and signed papers promising that they would never return to the area the crowd relented. The shaken men then traipsed the rest of the way to Corwen, where most of the town's population came out to see the police and those they had been unable to protect summarily bundled onto a waiting train which elicited great cheers and a display of 'intense ... national feelings' by the people.

As a result of the Llangwm riots warrants were issued for 31 men and 300 unnamed accomplices. And in February 1888 eight of the 'Llangwm Tithe Martyrs' were tried for 'riot, rout, and assault' at Ruthin. The presiding judge said that the defendants were undoubtedly guilty as charged, but, evidently mindful of the popular reaction that could follow any punishments that he cared to mete out, he declared that all the men had been led astray by others and he merely bound them over to keep the peace to the tune of £20 each.[202]

After Llangwm, the Chief Constable of Denbighshire determined not to repeat the mistake of providing inadequate manpower to deal with any potential disorders, which could have jeopardised the lives of his officers and did result in their humiliation. He was well aware that it was 'not desirable to call on the military till the civil strength has become exhausted', but he was prepared to use soldiers if necessary, and he soon had the opportunity to practice his new policy when some bailiffs were forcibly expelled from the countryside around 'Bodfair' (or Bodfari), on the Flintshire-Denbighshire border. The fact that the parson at Bodfari was subjected to 'parcels with loathsome contents and threatening letters' by non-conformist anti-tithers probably reinforced Major Leadbetter's belief that there would be trouble at a sale scheduled for 11 June 1887, and so he personally led the distraining party on that day accompanied by 50-60 policemen and two platoons (72 men) of the Cheshire Regiment under Major Hare. When the column arrived on the outskirts of the village lookouts blew horns and fired guns, just as their comrades at Llangwm and Mostyn had done, and about 100-200 people, some of them in possession of sticks and stones, soon appeared. They were joined by others en route to farms in the surrounding hills (but Mr Stephens' estimate that there were 1,000 people contradicts other witnesses' accounts that there were at most a few hundred individuals present), and at the first farm visited, Glan Clwyd, the people blocked the path of the security forces and stampeded cattle to prevent them from being seized for sale. A good deal of pushing and shoving ensued, followed by the usual fusillade of rotten eggs and 'a little stone throwing'.

After this skirmish the outsiders then proceeded to Tyn-y-celyn Farm, where more than 200 people caused a 'considerable amount of disorder'. The police and the protestors locked horns in a 'scrimmage' in which about 40 of the mob hurled sticks and stones at the police, and unusually one 'very violent man' was arrested by them. This probably stemmed both from the presence of the Chief Constable and the army contingent, whom the men doubtless wished to impress with their effectiveness, and the fact that the police wanted to reimpose some of their authority after the Llangwm fiasco. Indeed, another man who was throwing eggs at the police was surrounded by them, a journalist noted, and 'what eggs he had remaining were squashed in his pockets. Poor fellow. People kept at a respectable distance from him for the next hour or so'. The crowd was angered by the arrest of one of their own, however, and the dignity of the Constabulary was undermined once more when 'some of the police were ... drenched by an old woman with a dishful of water'. Moreover, a bull was released by one of the protestors amongst the spectating soldiers, and it forced them to 'scoot ... in all directions amidst derisive shouts and laughter'. Thereafter, the Chief Constable decided that discretion was the better part of valour and, rather than have Mr Justice Turnour read the Riot Act, he ordered the release of the miscreant and the withdrawal of his whole number from the area. The rabble barracked them as they left empty-handed and they had gained yet another victory over the authorities.[203]

News of this success soon got about, and the population of Denbigh was roused into 'the greatest activity' in the town. A mob assembled outside the lodgings of six bailiffs who were working from there, and they were dragged outside in an attempt to take them to the railway station for the 'ritual' of forcible repatriation. Four of the men somehow managed to escape their clutches, but the host still had two captives to work on, and both of them were beaten up and one was tossed into a local pond! The unfortunate duo then had to swear that they would never return to the town before they were shepherded onto the train and out of the county.[204]

In the light of these turbulent scenes, when a distraining expedition made its way to the St Asaph district to carry out a series of sales on 16 June 1887 it travelled with over 70 policemen and a similar number of soldiers who were available in reserve to deal with any trouble that got out of hand. When this cavalcade appeared near the cathedral city messages as to their whereabouts were sent from village to village, and large crowds massed at both Tremeirchion and St Asaph where there were some 'angry scenes'. At Y Waun Farm near St Asaph one woman scored a direct hit on ap Mwrog with a lump of turf to resounding cheers, and at other farms bailiffs were 'driven away'. However, the police reported that there was 'no great disturbance', and in these instances they were able to keep the peace without the military becoming involved at all.[205]

The rest of the day would not run so smoothly for the guardians of law and order, however, for they proceeded to take a train down the coast to Mochdre, and when they alighted at around 1.30*pm* the local people were ready for them. Chief Constable Leadbetter and his counterpart from Flintshire, Peter Browne, must have been confident that they could deter troublemakers from starting any real bother, having with them 76 policemen and 76 troops under Major Hare and Lieutenant Tucker from four companies of the Cheshires, who were 'in heavy marching order, with a full supply of ball cartridge'. But like some of their comrades, the Mochdre anti-tithe campaigners had prepared for their arrival in quasi-military fashion, having round-the-clock lookouts posted with signal equipment, organising a large force 'armed with long clubs and sticks' that could turn out in good order at a moment's notice and undertake 'well organised' resistance, and boasting leaders who had devised a 'concerted plan' of action.

Already the activists were well versed in their roles, having appeared in their hundreds at the village in response to an alarum (false as it turned out), on 13 June. Now, on the afternoon of 16 June, the sentries in the hills overlooking the settlement blew long horns, raised flags on the peaks and even fired several cannon. This activity warned everybody for miles around and must have surprised the security forces, who nonetheless headed straight for Mochdre, which they soon found to be 'in a state of siege'. An 'unruly mob' of 200-250 people awaited their arrival in the village, and up to 200 more set off in groups to alert the hill folk that their assistance was required. Farmers from nearby were soon lining up with five-foot-long wooden poles at the old mill on the Granllyn to Mochdre road, which was their predesignated meeting place, and within the next hour or two reinforcements from Colwyn Bay, Conwy and other towns and villages were heading for this spot. These 'mostly respectable people' booed and hassled the auctioneers and their assistants as they set off into the country, and Anti-Tithe League leaders like Howell Gee appealed to the commonalty for calm. But the ever-growing crowd was determined to prevent any sales by the 'foreigners' and to share in the glory of their fellow anti-tithers in Llangwm and elsewhere.

At Hugh Roberts' Mynydd Farm, Major Leadbetter spoke to the League's leaders in a bid to use their good offices to control the mob, who numbered perhaps 500 or more (although the auctioneer, ap Mwrog, later estimated their number to be around 3000), while the sales procedure was instituted. But, in spite of the League officials' worthy intentions, members of the gathering questioned the Major's authority and simply 'made fun of him'. Unperturbed, the Chief Constable sent 26 of his policemen towards a field to requisition some stock so that the auction could commence, but about 100 men with sticks swiftly moved across the lane and blocked access to it. More police were sent into the scrum that had begun between the two sides, and about another 150 joined the opposition to them. As the pushing and shoving developed into a violent fracas the 'mob became more and more unruly and the auctioneer was subjected to all manner of insult'. Some of the nationalistic gathering shouted for 'Home Rule!' and 'Mr Gladstone!', and although the troops from England had not engaged any of the Welsh farmers their presence must have heightened tensions and frayed tempers. Indeed, there was 'severe struggling going on' for quite some time, until the police were ordered, according to one of the crowd, Abel Hughes, to 'sweep the road entirely'. Whether or not this was the case, about 50 men and youths who stood on grassy banks overlooking the fray thought that the police were going to sweep the resistance to them aside by using their truncheons, and so they started to stone the police.

Another witness later asserted that the Constabulary then 'made a fierce attack on the Anti-Tithers ... (with) their staves ... (and they) seemed for a time to have lost their usual coolness'. The rabble were also guilty of upping the ante at this point, because over and above the usual eggs and stones they hurled sharpened sticks and reportedly used sling shot. Some of the farmers even charged into the police on their horses led by an ex-cavalryman, T H Jones, and Major Leadbetter admitted that 'blows were given and taken' on both sides. For several minutes 'the fighting was furious', and a journalist wrote that 'the affair bore the resemblance of a battle'. One rioter, John Roberts, a builder from Colwyn Bay, said that he was kicked 'very violently' by the police and that one constable assaulted his father with his baton. At this, Mr Roberts recounted, he told the PC that he would report him to the Chief Constable, to which he replied 'thou shalt have it (too), thou devil'. Roberts added that about a dozen of the throng were 'bleeding terribly' from head wounds, and they and others were 'in an insensible condition'. One of them was the farmers' leader Eli Hughes, who had his 'skull ... cracked and his arm broken' by the 'Bobbie'. In all, about 50 people were injured by the police during the riot, many of the casualties being taken to the Ty Felin Mill, where the floors were saturated with blood by the end of the afternoon.

The rioters were not the only ones to suffer during the Mochdre riot either, for 34 policemen, half from Denbighshire and half from Flintshire, received wounds from the mob, some of them serious head injuries caused by a 'very thick' rain of rocks and other debris that fell upon them. The Deputy Chief Constable of Flintshire, Mr Bolton, concurred with other witnesses that felons 'were throwing tremendous stones' and that many of the police thought that they 'would have been killed' by them. Even Major Leadbetter was struck and 'plastered all over the head with cow dung', and so it was something of a tribute to the forbearance of senior officers and the rank-and-file that the military were not called in in these circumstances. Fortunately after some minutes the crowd withdrew to lick its wounds, and at this point the auction men were able to come out of hiding from the hedgerows and compel farmer Roberts to pay his tithe.

The Mochdre rioters were not content to let the distraining party continue their work unhindered, however, and when their 'foe' moved off to a second farm at Felin Gate groups of men behind the hedges adjacent to the road showered them with 'huge stones hurled with great force'. Indeed, the magistrate present, Mr A A Walker, warned the masses that if they did not stop their unlawful activities and disperse forthwith he would feel obliged to read the Riot Act. His words had no effect, and it took another police baton charge to make the opposition desist and afford the party a relatively trouble-free passage to a third farm at Peurallt Isa (Tanrallt Ucha). The police had not managed to shake off their unwanted followers by the time that the auctioneer prepared for another sale here, and as several hundred people milled about the farm in a menacing fashion the Magistrate's Clerk, Oliver George of Abergele, begged Mr Walker to read the Riot Act to pre-empt any further rioting. One of the assemblage, John Roberts, later related that he tried to tell Mr George that such action was not warranted, but he replied 'Pooh, Pooh' and despite some misgivings, the Magistrate read the Riot Act which was translated into Welsh by Sergeant Lewis of Abergele. At last 'this had a quieting effect' upon the riff raff and the sale went ahead without further hindrance, and thereafter the representatives of authority in this case were able to withdraw having achieved their objectives.[206]

The riots during the middle of 1887 brought the anti-tithe campaign national press and parliamentary attention and also led to a government enquiry into them chaired by Mr John Bridge, a Metropolitan Police magistrate. This indicates both their intensity and the concern felt about them by the powers-that-be, coming as they did at a time of grave anxiety about the 'Home Rulers' of Scotland, and especially of Ireland, for the last thing that the Westminster government wanted at this juncture was the development of a third front in Wales. As the Anti-Tithe League leadership capitalised on the publicity generated by the riots and focussed the movement's attention on political agitation, 'the second half of 1887 was relatively quiet'. But the Clwyd Record Office account's assertion that 'generally speaking open violence no longer took place' brushes over numerous anti-tithe disturbances in the area.[207] Although there was less violence, in December 1887 there were fresh disorders in Flintshire when distraint sales were attempted. Clashes occurred at Tanrallt Farm near Holywell, and at Ffordd Hir Farm in Gwernaffield, near Mold, when 'a crowd of roughs with large sticks in their hands assembled' at the property owned by J S Bankes of Sychdyn Hall. They prevented the Church Agent, Thomas Jones of Coed Du, and Mr E W I Peterson of the London-based Church Defence Association, from carrying out a survey of the holding, and they forcibly ejected them from the land. There was a 'considerable altercation' too at Lakefield in Caergwrle , when a distraining party tried to take away cattle, and some of the 'common herd' gathered to blow whistles and horns, and to block the police and to destroy effigies of them.[208]

Agitation over the tithe continued in Flintshire in the New Year, and on 8 January 1888 about 60 men of the 13th Hussars from Manchester arrived in Holywell to support the police when they attended a number of distraints in the farming belt around the town. They were 'completely accoutred for the field' and added to the tense atmosphere in Holywell created by the presence of between 12 and 20 paramilitary 'emergency men' with experience of Ireland and service in the cavalry, and bailiffs, who also were to assist at the sales. Once these forces had been marshalled they were accompanied by about 50 policemen from Flintshire, Denbighshire and Caernarfonshire, and the auctioneers, to various steads outside Holywell. The column was followed by anti-tithe 'agitators in vehicles of all descriptions' including horse-drawn carts, carriages, and lorries, while messengers alerted the farmers about the impending arrival of 'the enemy'. At Pentre Ffynnon Farm, Charles Stephens, the Church Agent, was harangued by a large rabble armed with sticks, and a reporter noted that 'the witty element was of course to the fore'. Anti-Tithe League leaders such as Howell Gee and Tom Ellis MP appealed for calm though, and the presence of the soldiery 'cowed' the mob. Nonetheless, a nasty incident was only narrowly averted when an alert police constable spotted and stopped 'a lad in the act of inserting a fuse in a large log of wood in which he had placed a quantity of blasting powder'.[209] Had he not been apprehended the first fatalities of the 'Tithe War' could have resulted either from the explosion or the military response that probably would have followed it.

Flintshire quietened down somewhat during 1888 after this scare, but just over the county line at Llanferres in Denbighshire 'there was a (good) deal of uproar and rowdyism' on 10 April, and the distraining agent and a bailiff were seized by a non-conformist mob and 'baptised in a pool of cow's filth. All sorts of horns were blown, drums beaten (and) the noise was (said to be) almost unbearable … (but eventually) the farmer's wife paid the tithe, and then gave the tithe collector a blow on his face, for which she received deafening cheers'.[210]

Only a week or so after the Llanferres disturbance, on 18 April, the police returned to the site of their greatest ignominy to date, Llangwm, and 80 of them had to face hostile crowds bent on causing them grief. They successfully conducted distraints there without giving rise to disorders on anything like the scale of a year before though, and Chief Constable Leadbetter complimented them on the restraint that they had shown on this occasion.[211] But, in spite of the police force's concerted efforts not to provoke the anti-tithe lobby they could do little about the underlying causes of unrest, and as pressures built up once more in sections of the Denbighshire farming community it was only a matter of time before they were vented.

On 9 May 1888 the police had to deal with numbers of people who converged on the *Royal*

Oak public house in Denbigh, where several bailiffs were being put up, with the intention of attacking them. They barged into the building and searched for the men in vain, and this should have alerted the police to the possibility of further trouble at sales that the officials were to work at on the following day. Yet on 10 May Mr Stephens and his associates were guarded by only two constables on their excursion to Llanefydd (Llannefydd), just outside Denbigh, compared to the 80 men sent to Llangwm. Senior officers doubtless saw no reason to think that this village would be a flashpoint like Llangwm, and after the relative lull in rioting since Mochdre they may have harboured a belief that violence was less likely to be used by the population now. In addition, the Chief Constable's revised 'general policy ... to send as few men as possible (was adopted) partly to reduce the cost to the ratepayers (of policing scores of distraints), and also to prevent accusations that too many men were being deliberately sent to (them to) antagonise the local people'. The decision to send what turned out to be an 'inadequate police escort' to Llannefydd allowed a riotous situation to develop there, and 'a large mob of several hundred' persons chased the distrainers from farm to farm and eventually, tail between their legs, back into Denbigh. A few days later, on 16 May, Mr Stephens *et al* returned to Llannefydd with Superintendent Vaughan, eleven other policemen and seven 'emergency men'. But as soon as they appeared horns were sounded and big crowds blocked their path, and 'the resistance and menacing of (this) ... large mob became so violent that (Superintendent Vaughan) ... considered it advisable' to make a swift exit.

On 17 May, the Chief Constable personally headed a squad of 33 police officers that marched into Llannefydd, only to be confronted by a well prepared and forewarned mob of about 600, including labourers from Denbigh, Llansannan and other villages who acted 'in a thoroughly organised manner'. After suffering a good deal of abuse, the police proceeded to Nant Isaf farm, where, according to Major Leadbetter, 'the conduct of the mob ... was even more impudent and aggressive' than before, and at Bryn Gwyn farm the rabble became very 'disorderly'. Men carrying large sticks charged into the police and women threw stones at them, and 40 or 50 people accosted Mr Stephens to prevent him from beginning the sale. They used hooters and banged trays and the iron roofs of out-buildings to drown him out, and 'the noise made was truly deafening'. One of the protest leaders, William Jones (whose mother was standing nearby with a black flag, in the manner of the Llangwm 'Martyrs'), then stood right next to Mr Stephens and beat a metal tray at his ear, and apparently this led to scuffling and a 'sudden, sharp and severe incident' in which 'blows were struck' by both factions. The Chief Constable recalled afterwards that he responded to the 'disgraceful' behaviour by the 'most aggressive and threatening element' of the mob by ordering his man to protect the sales officials, and they drew their truncheons and a 'fierce fight' got under way. A journalist graphically described the 'catastrophe' that resulted, with the police charging into the masses, some of whom recoiled while others 'stood their ground in a manner which was surprising'. Many of them 'were beaten about the head in a most appaling manner, the contact of the staves with the heads causing a sickening sound, felling them to the ground or causing them to fly in all directions bleeding and screaming with pain'. About 25 people were wounded by the police batons, and more than half received 'ghastly scalp wounds (that had) ... blood gushing out (of them) in torrents'. The rioters withdrew to tend to their casualties at this point and the disturbances for that day were at an end.

In spite of this bloody conflagration, however, on 18 May hundreds of rowdy demonstrators made their feelings against the police known, when 80 of them visited numerous farms near Llannefydd in a fresh attempt to undertake distraint sales there. The Chief Constable appreciated that there was 'bad feeling' in the air and that the people were spoiling for another fight, and when the police, bailiffs and several 'emergency men' armed with guns found themselves in a hollow at Simdde Hir, and surrounded on all sides by the baying mob, the Riot Act was read. Anti-Tithe league leaders including Howell Gee urged the crowds to disperse before the 'enemy' opened fire on them, and only their intervention prevented another bloody incident.

On returning to Denbigh later that day, Major Leadbetter reflected on recent events and 'in view of the increasing strain on the limited resources of the police force' he requested a detachment of troops to assist him, and men of the 9th Lancers arrived in the town from Manchester on 23 May. It appears that by this time the Chief Constable and the local magistrates had lost patience with the Anti-Tithe League leaders who attended distraints at which his men were continuously abused and attacked, and on the day that the soldiers arrived in Denbigh, the Clerk to the Magistrates, John Parry-Jones, posted up an order that no groups of four or more people (the minimum number in law who could engage specifically in riot), would be allowed in future to 'assembl(e) together and conduct ... themselves in a turbulent and disorderly manner' in the district. In addition, Major Leadbetter issued his men with a new General Order that, henceforth, police officers were to have no contact with either leaders of the Anti-Tithe League or any 'hostile members of the crowd'. Furthermore, they would be equipped with 'leggings, great coats or capes' when attending any events at which trouble may occur. E R Edwards has asserted that the security forces 'met no resistance' in the course of their duties in the following weeks,[212] but the anti-tithers of the Denbigh area were still ready to test them on occasion.

The day after the cavalry had arrived in Denbigh, 24 May 1888, they were called upon to assist the police at the village of Llansannan, just outside the town. The Chief Constable and his men were once again trying to afford Mr Stephens and his entourage the opportunity to gather tithes in the locale and up to 2000 people appeared to see the train of 'several conveyances' led by the mounted soldiers who 'were heartily cheered everywhere (while) ... the police were heartily groaned at'. When the distrainers made off for some nearby granges the familiar wall of sound from horns, pots and pans and the like burst forth, 'to drown (out) the auctioneer's voice', and he and his men were jostled by their audience at Clwt Farm. As violence broke out, the new no-nonsense approach of the powers-that-be was instigated, with the Lancers lined up ready for the Riot Act to be read by a magistrate. One of the Anti-Tithe League leaders, the solicitor, Mr A Lloyd, called on his following to come to their senses, while 'the Major threatened to charge them'. Indeed, when some individuals continued to assault the auction party the Lancers 'made a feint charge and everybody had to scramble through a thick hedgerow' out of the path of the horses. But this effectively extinguished the mob's desire to oppose the distraint, and when the soldiers returned to their holding position the sale went ahead. In fact, after this the protestors had a whip-round for the troopers to pay for their refreshments, while they vented their frustration by smashing the windows of the house occupied by the village policeman, PC Davies. Clearly it was only the unusual active participation of the military in the anti-tithe events at Llansannan that prevented even worse trouble from occurring that day, and after this test of wills the local population decided to avoid another head-to-head with them while they remained in the vicinity (which was until the end of June 1888).[213]

For much of the rest of 1888 the anti-tithers of north-east Wales took a break from their energetic brand of physical force campaigning and adhered to the appeals of more moderate voices in the movement who wished to avoid any further interventions by the army with the innate risks of bloodshed that they entailed. The underlying tensions in the region did not disappear, however, and there were sporadic bouts of disorder in Flintshire and Denbighshire. On 29 June 1888, at a troublesome distraint in Caerwys, a mock altar and an effigy of a vicar greeted officials visiting Ty Ucha Farm, and the local bishop, the Rev A G Edwards of St Asaph, noted that his colleagues often had similar 'personal insults and outrages inflicted upon (them)'. As well as burned effigies, they received threatening letters, had their vicarage doors tarred, and they were constantly put in fear of attack. Indeed, the Bishop asserted that 'more than one clergyman died under th(e) ... combined strain' of this onslaught by the anti-tithe faction,[214] and if this is the case they were the first and only fatalities of the Tithe War.

Notwithstanding, there was very nearly another death late in December 1888 at a farm near Ruthin, when Mr C E Jones, a Church Agent, went to collect a tithe payment with an associate and a policeman. Apparently the disgruntled farmer appeared at the door with a shotgun and 'pointed it ... at the head of the agent (who) ... to avoid ... the probable consequences ... (gallantly) slipped behind the policeman who accompanied him'! Before the farmer was able to discharge his weapon, however, the three men had scarpered and they then ran back to Denbigh.[215]

During 1889 there were fewer violent incidents than in previous years as developments outside Wales affected the attitudes of its people. The Anglican church made an effort to reform the system of tithe payments and three Bills relating to issues raised by the anti-tithe movement were considered over the course of the parliament. Above and beyond these initiatives a new Welsh Education Act was passed by Westminster, which relieved some of the pressures on the Establishment, and an upturn in the economy had a similarly beneficial effect in respect to the position in north-east Wales. Additionally, the Anti-Tithe League's leaders continued to make pleas for a concentration of local energies on peaceful means of dissent,[216] and by and large these were respected.

On New Year's Day 1889 there was a recurrence of 'rowdy' mobbing at Llanferres, however, when an effigy of the vicar was decimated by his Non Conformist parishioners. And at a tithe sale near Llanfihangel Glyn Myfyr on 29 March two religious effigies were burned by protestors.[217] After these isolated incidents though, the authorities were given no further reasons to worry until 1890.

On 1 January 1890, on the anniversary of the disturbances at Llanferres a year before, six Calvinistic preachers drew large audiences who caused uproar and paraded another effigy of the rector. A similar effigy of the parish priest of Derwen, the Rev M Hughes, was burned on 17th. April 1890 by a mob that mocked the Church of England and threatened to kill it's local representative, and then engaged in 'tithe riots' in the area.[218] Moreover, there was friction during the summer months at a village that had 'gained wide notoriety' for anti-tithe violence by this stage – Llannefydd.

In the second week of June 1890 the long-suffering and much-maligned Mr Stephens and his band of helpers travelled around Llannefydd and attempted to hold distraints at numerous

locations. As before, they were prevented from achieving their aims by the local anti-tithe 'warriors', and so Stephens' crew returned to the area a week later, around 18 June, with two policemen and two 'emergency men'. On approaching Henllan the Commissioners' agent heard a gunshot warning the community of their intrusion, and about 20 villagers immediately declaimed against them. They managed to negotiate their way to a nearby farm without trouble, but at a second horns were blown and by the time that they arrived at Pen-y-frith hill farm (at over 1,000 feet above sea-level), up to 100 people were banging trays, pots and-cans, and 'rattling buildings *etc* with sticks'. A journalist recorded the fact that the noise was 'incessant (and) ... deafening', and that Mr Stephens was physically obstructed at the farm gates. He and the men with him therefore headed for Tyn-y-pistyll, where the unfortunate agent had 'a dozen tithe horns ... placed close to his ears' and blown, and after a final unsuccessful attempt to hold an auction at Pantyronnen farm the distraining party withdrew. As they made off, however, some of the mob got entangled in a scuffle with them, and a bucket was thrown at the distrainer's horses. The heavily outnumbered 'emergency men' responded by using their staffs, and 'the wildest disorder' followed as blows were exchanged and stones thrown, and Mr Stephens and his associates were chased out of the neighbourhood back towards Denbigh. Later that day the rioters paraded triumphantly through Henllan, where most of the village enthusiastically cheered them, and on hearing of this latest 'disgrace' Chief Constable Leadbetter let it be known that if there was any recurrence of such behaviour he would swiftly secure a troop of Hussars to quell this dissension.[219]

The inhabitants of Llannefydd paid heed to Major Leadbetter's warning only until 11 August 1890, when Mr Stephens ventured to the village once more, along with a Church Commissioner, Mr Dale, two 'emergency men' and a dozen police. Howell Gee did his best to keep the masses under control when the expedition entered the locality, but many of them brandished sticks and cudgels, and as the police tried to get to Nant Farm the 'excited mob (displayed their intense) detestation ... (of the police) ... in a savage manner'. First they blocked the path of the authorities' carriages and banged pots and pans and blew so many horns that they 'sounded like a large number of steamers using their foghorns'. Then when they had drawn the police out into the open they allowed them to make their way through the throng to the farm gates. It was here that the police realised that they had been lulled into a trap, for the gates were locked and tarred with thorns, and as the seething crowd tried to envelop them and rained down blows upon them the officers beat a hasty retreat to the carriages and ordered a speedy departure.[220] When Superintendent Vaughan reported this riot to his superior, Chief Constable Leadbetter immediately requested military aid, and a detachment of the 10th Hussars arrived at Denbigh by special train from York soon afterwards.

A week after the first disturbances at Llannefydd, on 18 August, the Major led a body of 12 policemen, 44 soldiers under Captains Cole and Mesham, two mounted 'emergency men' and two in a brake with the sales men and magistrates, into the opposition's territory. They were followed in horse-drawn traps by Anti-Tithe League leaders including Gwilym Parry and

---

Facing: Troopers of the 10th Hussars relaxing at their camp near Denbigh during the 'Tithe War' of 1890.

Howell Gee, and when the whole convoy neared Henllan horns were blown and what one witness described as a large 'pagan mob' materialised before them. Some of the women present used 'foul language ... not to be expected from any but the lowest class' towards the police, but when the constables tried to arrest some of the multitude they all ran off. The convoy then pressed on into the countryside, and at one farm the police and the locals engaged in a good deal of pushing and shoving which culminated in them quite comically bursting through the doors of a barn and quickly filling it up. As the hordes within piled out of the building a number of policemen and locals clambered over a gate, and a reporter on the spot said that Mr Parry, one of the Anti-Tithe League leaders, pushed the gate and it landed on one PC Wyse's foot. He and an 'emergency man' then rapidly 'threw down the gate, Mr Gwilym Parry being thrown down with it, the gate being upon him, and one policeman actually put his foot on the gate'. The journalist continued that 'it was ludicrous to see nearly every man in the crowd put down on a bit of paper the constable's number'. Indeed, following 'loud protests' about the incident to the Chief Constable by the mob, Major Leadbetter felt obliged to make a public apology for his men's action and he assured them that there would be no further violence perpetrated on his side.

Calm was soon restored, but at the next farm on the Church Agent's list a number of calves were destined to be sold, and they first had to be caught. When the bailiffs tried to take hold of them dozens of people ran among the cattle, ably assisted by six excited sheep-dogs, and soon half-a-dozen Hussars and as many police had joined in the chase. In view of their lack of success in capturing the stock, other 'Hussars spurred their chargers and were in hot pursuit' with lassos, and the Chief Constable and the soldiers joined the crowd in 'indulging in a hearty laugh at their own expense'.

This good-humoured duelling also went on at the next property visited for distraint, where the farm gates had been blockaded and liberally coated with tar, thorns and wire. The police and emergency men shrugged their shoulders and set about chopping up the obstruction, covering themselves in tar in the process, which delighted the onlookers including 'the Hussars (who) sat laughing at the proceedings, which were extremely ludicrous'. When the police had completed their sticky task, however, Mr Stephens began to conduct another sale, and some women armed with sticks threatened both him and the police surrounding him, and stones, sticks and clods of earth were showered upon them. The presence of the soldiers ensured that this battery only lasted for a short time though, and sales were carried out successfully later on that day, and on 19 and 20 August Indeed, by the end of the month eight persons were charged with a breach of the peace on 11 August, and although those who rioted in the following days seem to have been more fortunate, the arrests had the effect of quietening the notoriously rebellious community for the time being.[221]

Facing: Men of the 10th Hussars under the command of Captain Onslow and Lieutenant Farquarson, at Denbigh, August 1890 about to leave to escort a distraining party during the 'Tithe War'. The two figures standing on the left are Mr Windsor Davies, JP and the Chief Constable of Denbighshire, Major Leadbetter. Superintendent Vaughan is standing in front of the mounted civilian on the right of the rear line of troopers. The figure holding the reins of the carriage on the right is Mr Stephens with Mr Clarke standing in front wearing a light coloured cap. [Denbighshire Record Office]

Not surprisingly, the final disturbances of the Tithe War were also at Llannefydd. A Mr Croft of Mold went to the village with the intent of collecting tithe payments and although he had applied in advance to the Chief Constable of Denbighshire for a police escort, Major Leadbetter had refused his request because he considered that there was no longer any danger of the natives becoming restless there. But, on 30 December 1890, Mr Croft 'was met by a large and angry crowd and he was compelled' to leave the area without making any collections. On the following day he returned with Superintendent Vaughan and 35 police officers, and this time his objectives were achieved without having to face the wrath of the rabble. Yet the local populace retained their defiance, and when more distraints were held at Llannefydd on 12 January 1891 the auctioneers required the protection of three-dozen policemen. Even then the 'crowds were large and noisy' and pockets of violent protest led to charges of breaching the peace, and 'but for the police no sales could have been effected'.[222]

Soon after these final tithe disorders, on 24 March 1891, a new Tithe Recovery Act was passed by Parliament, and this made landlords liable for payment of the tithe rather than their tenants. Although there was a loop-hole, in that unscrupulous landlords could simply raise their tenants' rents to take account of the increased tithe charge, violent 'anti-tithe agitation ... (soon) evaporated', and although large crowds still turned up at distraints when some tenants refused to pay their higher rents, the Liberal Government took up the 'Land Question' and the issue of the Dis-establishment of the Church in Wales, and eventually both of these points were resolved to the satisfaction of the Welsh people, which was in good measure a result of the tithe riots and protests. [223]

Industrial and other disturbances, 1893-1915

Early in 1893 another economic depression hit the industrial north-east of Wales and, in addition to sacking 150 miners, the owners of the Powell & Drowsall Seams Blast Pit in Brymbo proposed a 25% wage cut for their men. On 29 July they went out on strike, and although they returned to work *en masse* on 18 October, 'there was rioting and damage (inflicted) at Westminster colliery' a week later when their colleagues also withdrew their labour. Indeed, the 14th Hussars had to be called in from Wrexham to control the area's striking colliers, who stoned the police with slag and other debris, and the rioting was only halted when an old and respected constable spoke to the mob in Welsh and persuaded them to desist. There was trouble over wage cuts at Buckley as well, where 700 men walked out and then marched on Leeswood 'to destroy property and to prevent work' being done by other miners, and only the presence of a large contingent of police forestalled disturbances there. The police also were required to intervene when north Wales quarrymen downed tools and caused disorders during the 1890s,[224] and Buckley was the scene of the last disturbances of the 19th century.

On 8 August 1893, Major J M Gibson had acquired a 50-year lease on three acres of Buckley Common from Mr Peter Davies-Cooke of Gwysaney, with the aim of using it as a drilling ground for the Buckley Volunteer force. Gibson arranged for them to drain the land and to erect a seven foot high iron fence around it, which was done during the spring of 1894.

But on 7 May that year the local non-conformist minister, the Rev Joseph Davies, organised a group of friends into a Commons Defence Association that could protect the rights of all those who wished to use the land. One week later they rallied at the common and broke down the enclosure fences, which were soon rebuilt by the Volunteers, and various other buildings were raised on the site over the following months. On 16 October, the Association gathered a group of 300-400 people, some of them with hammers, axes and crowbars, to demolish the fences and other structures, and about 40 of them and the Reverend set about their task with gusto. A watchman who had seen the mob approaching and gone to get help returned to the field with three policemen, but they could do little and simply watched as the crowd razed the fences and buildings. And although the outraged Major Gibson later took some of the perpetrators to court, it found in favour of the people and upheld their rights. 225

The Flintshire police once more went into the breach in 1910, at Hawarden, where disorder broke out during an industrial dispute at Hawarden Bridge Iron Works' sheet mills. In the spring of 1910 mass pickets tried to prevent strike-breakers from entering the premises, and the police were deployed to allow them to do so, and to guard the Works and the area around it. On the night of 6 April, about 70 strikers armed 'with sticks or weapons' including truncheons, rolling pins and hammers, tried to enter the Works offices by force, and they were confronted by 19 Flintshire police and 35 of their fellow officers from Lancashire. Several of

A group of potential rioters (escorted by two police officers) approaching Brynkinallt Colliery during the 1912 disturbances. [W A Williams Collection]

Men of the Suffolk Regiment face the disgruntled miners at Brynkinallt Colliery, 1912.
[W A Williams Collection]

the constables reported that a 'tumultuous' fracas erupted and that during it one of the strikers cried 'Don't push or I'll put a hole through you!'. A number of the strikers were injured in the scuffle, although the police insisted that 'no staffs (were) drawn' by them, and 15 of the assailants were arrested because of their 'threatening attitude'.[226] Later on that year, on 5 December, some of the strikers decided to return to work, and they had to be escorted in by two-dozen policemen through the ranks of angry pickets. Their numbers gradually swelled to 1800, and so the Chief Constable of Flintshire called in 110 more reinforcements from Warrington, Manchester and across Lancashire. On 8 December, as the police tried to ferry workers into the plant, they were obstructed by about 500 men and clashes occurred that almost led to 'a very serious disturbance'. The police quickly managed to quash the trouble though, and on the following day only about 70 die-hards attempted to block their path. Thereafter, the police negotiated with one of the strike leaders, James Walker, in an attempt to stop any more mass pickets and the violence associated with them, and the last of these was staged on 16 December. Indeed, Walker's Associated Iron and Steel Workers' Union members all returned to the works without any fuss on 18 January 1911.[227]

But, the Smelters' Union remained at loggerheads with the management until the summer of 1911. On 10 July, when some of the smelters also tried to return to work, they were 'compelled ... to return home (by a large crowd) and a workman was struck in the face'. This incident did not lead to any immediate escalation in the level of violence, but the threat of a return to work evidently infuriated the strikers, and when that day's shift changed at 10*pm* 'suddenly, without the slightest warning, the picket burst passed the police' into the works. The 800 or so invaders were 'extremely noisy' and soon put a stop to production, and they menacingly searched out strike-breaking 'strangers ... (and generally) became very demonstrative'. The Chief Constable of Flintshire, Mr J I Davies, reflected the day after this incident that 'outbreaks (of violence had become) ... so numerous and spontaneous during the last 18 months that it has been a matter of utter impossibility to deal with them in a proper manner', and he wondered whether it may now be time to call upon the assistance of the Military Power.[228]

In the event, there were no repeats of the disorders at Hawarden later that year, but in 1912 the coal miners' unions organised their first national strike, and there were demonstrations at Ruabon, Cefn Mawr and other pits during the first few months of 1912. Moreover, when the men of the Brynkinallt pit near Chirk carried on working it became the focus for hundreds of pickets armed with sticks and cudgels from Cefn and other pits in the surrounding district, and a 'large body of police' required back-up from the army, which was provided by the Suffolk Regiment. During March 1912 the pit became the scene of bitter confrontation between the two sides, and so the owner, Mr Craig, spoke to the crowds and urged them not to provoke 'the riot squads' encamped on nearby parkland. After a little scuffling and a lot of heckling the demonstrators decided that they should heed his advice, and they dispersed without the military having to be embroiled in the situation.[229]

The final riot in the period up to the end of the First World War,[230] was actually a manifestation of anti-German feelings harboured by much of the populace at this time. Such sentiments were heightened by the sinking of the *Lusitania* by a German U-boat on 4 May 1915, and there were riots in Liverpool soon afterwards, directed against naturalised Germans living in the city. On 7 May, anti-German demonstrations were held in several Welsh towns, including Rhyl, where the Welsh Regiment were billeted, and they were put on alert for spies. Two weeks later, one of its patrols picked up a Mr Arthur R Brougham following a report from Mrs Ada Rayner that he had told her 'it will not be long before Kinmel Park (Army) Camp will be blown up'. In the light of Brougham's odd refusal to divulge his name and nationality to the patrol's Sergeant he was taken into military custody, and 'a large crowd followed the prisoner ... chiefly ... soldiers', many of whom it transpired were out on the town and were 'drunk at the time'. The suspect was taken for interrogation to Rhyl police station, outside which a large number of people congregated, and there the Welsh Regiment's Commanding Officer arranged for Dr A E Lloyd to examine the man, whom, the physician proclaimed, was 'not insane, but peculiar'. Dissatisfied with the lack of news about the suspect, 'several attempts were made by the (drunken) soldiers to break into the police station through the windows, but (they) were prevented (from entering) by the police and special constables (all of whom were) ... roughly handled and assaulted'. When a General appeared and ordered them back to barracks (which were near the promenade), however, most of the khaki revellers did so. But, at 9.15 p.m., the rest of the restless multitude proceeded to 35, Queen Street, the home of Robert Fassy, a naturalised Swiss-German immigrant, and he and his wife Edith and their two infants suffered the wrath of the mob. Their barber's shop was ransacked and all the windows of their premises smashed by the rioters, who inflicted over

£45 worth of damage. Furthermore, they forced the Fassy family to flee, with Mr Fassy escaping as Mr Woods had done at Ruabon in 1830 by dressing up as a woman! In 1917 he laid claims for 'damages caused by rioting' and theft totalling a loss of £110, and at the end of the War he received compensation for the 'anti-German riots at Rhyl'.[231] This was the last in a long list of violent civil protests in north-east Wales from the Acts of Union up to the end of the Great War, and with over 250 recorded riots (and doubtless many others that were unrecorded or which have yet to come to light), it is fair to say that the area was one of the most turbulent, community-conscious and forcefully active ones in the whole country.

Notes

1. See Chronology of Riots and Ructions in north-east Wales, 1536-1918, **pp7-9**.

2. Until April 1996, the area under consideration in this book and referred to as north-east Wales was the county of Clwyd. After that date it was divided among the unitary authorities of Denbighshire, Flintshire, Conwy and Wrexham. Of the incidents of fatalities in riots, G Rude, *The Crowd in History*, p 6. The dates for this study were chosen to cover the period of Welsh history from the seminal Acts of Union to the end of the Great War. On disturbances after 1918, see for example, J Putkowski *The Kinmel Park Riots, 1919*. The Great Civil War and other rebellions fall outside the scope of this work: for a more detailed definition of these and other terms relating to various forms of armed conflict see, T L Jones *The development of British counter-insurgency policies and doctrine, 1945-52*, Ch 2.

3. See list of Riots and Ructions in north-east Wales, 1536-1918, pp7-9.

4. See list of Riots and Ructions in north-east Wales, 1536-1918, pp7-9.

5. See list of Riots and Ructions in north-east Wales, 1536-1918, pp7-9.

6. On rioting before the 20th century, Rude pp6, 10-11, 34, 70, 242, 246, 255.

7. GM Griffiths,'Glimpses of Denbighshire in the records of the Court of Great Sessions', *Denbighshire Historical Society Transactions (DHST)*, 22 (1973) pp94-5. Rioting in Denbigh is listed in *Denbighshire Historical Society Quarter Sessions Indexes*.

8. Court of Quarter Sessions Records for old Denbighshire and old Flintshire are at the relevant County Record Offices. Unfortunately, though, there are no subject indexes for Flintshire to guide the researcher to references about cases of rioting. For Denbigh see *ff* 7 above. On the work of the Quarter Sessions and other courts, GD Owen *Elizabethan Wales*, p179.

9. GM Griffith pp93-4; M Salmon *A source book of Welsh history*, p 287. The National Library of Wales, Aberystwyth (NLW), published an Index to their Records of the Court of Great Sessions in 1995, but again it contains no specific listing for riot or other public disorders that could be used to identify references in the mass of records.

10. I ab O Edwards (Ed) *A catalogue of Star Chamber proceedings relating to Wales*, pp iii-iv.

11. I ab O Edwards (Ed) piv; Salmon p283; W L Williams *The making of modern Wales*, p103; GD Owen p 35.

12. For more detailed descriptions of all these institutions see the *Encyclopedia Brittanica*. A mass of material produced by these bodies is held at the Public Record Office, Kew, and future research may glean additional details from this source.

13. Earlier 'forcible entries' onto land occurred at, for example, Kinnerton, in the reign of (IRO) King Henry VII, I ab O Edwards (Ed) p1; and at Iscoyd and Droitwich, c1515-18; Northop, c1518-29; E A Lewis (Ed) *An inventory of early Chancery proceedings relating to Wales*, p111-13. See also P Warner *Famous Welsh battles*, p110-11.

14. On Denbigh, CAJ Skeel, *The Council in the Marches of Wales*, p.66. The rioters apparently declared that in future they would 'pay no stillage', which presumably was some type of tax paid to the English authorities. (The OED's first recorded use of the word is in 1596, and this refers to the storage of beer on stills.)

15. EA Lewis (ed), p80.

16. EA Lewis/J.C. Davies (eds), *Records of the Court of Argumentations relating to Wales and Monmouthshire*, p69.

17. EA Lewis/JC Davies (eds), p78.

18. *ibid*, p78.

19. *ibid*, p88.

20. I ab O Edwards (ed), p5.

21. EA Lewis (ed), pp94-95.

22. I ab O Edwards (ed), p17.

23. On the introduction and impact of enclosures, ST Bindoff, *Tudor England*, pp22-24. On various other reasons for popular disorders between the 13th and 16th centuries, Skeel, pp13 15, 212, 262.

24. I ab O Edwards (ed), p57.

25. I ab O Edwards (ed), p60. There was also a 'forcible entry' onto land at Ffridd Celynen in Llanrwst during 1574, but this part of old Denbighshire is now in Gwynedd.

26. R Flenley (ed), *A calendar of the register of the Queen's Majesty's Council in the Marches of Wales*, pp177-78.

27. I ab O Edwards (ed), p66.

28. GD Owen, p179.

29. Skeel, p101.

30. I ab O Edwards (ed), p71.

31. *ibid*, p62.

32. Flenley (ed), p227; GD Owen, p102.

33. GD Owen, p185.

34. GD Owen, pp156-57; EG Jones (ed), *Exchequer Proceedings (Equity) concerning Wales, Henry VIII to Elizabeth I*, p196.

35. GD Owen, pp172, 217-18.

36. EG Jones (ed), p150.

37. I ab O Edwards (ed), p56.

38. *ibid*, p58.

39. EG Jones (ed), p154.

40. I ab O Edwards (ed), p58.

41. *ibid*, p68.

42. *ibid*, p63.

43. *ibid*, p64.

44. *ibid*, p66.

45. *ibid*, p65.

46. On Denbigh, I ab O Edwards (ed), p63; on Llandegla and football riots, pp58, 63; AH Dodd *Studies in Stuart Wales*, p19.

47. EG Jones (ed), p161.

48. I ab O Edwards (ed), p68; Dodd, Studies, p19; *The Industrial Revolution in North Wales*, p75 (hereafter labelled as *Industrial*), p54.

49. I ab O Edwards (ed), p59.

50. *ibid*, pp63, 69.

51. *ibid*, p60.

52. EG Jones (ed) pp162-63.

53. I ab O Edwards (ed) p74.

54. EG Jones (ed), p166.

55. I ab O Edwards (ed), p64.

56. *ibid*, p56.

57. *ibid*, p66.

58. *ibid*, p93.

59. *ibid*, p56.

60. *ibid*, p66.

61. *ibid*, p56.

62. *ibid*, p70. Records of the Denbigh Workhouse can be found at the National Library of Wales.

63. *ibid*, p60.

64. *ibid*, p64.

65. *ibid*, p57.

66. I ab O Edwards (ed), p71.

67. GD Owen, p113.

68. I ab O Edwards (ed), p67; Dodd, *Industrial* [1971], p54.

69. I ab O Edwards (ed), p58.

70. Evan Francis Papers, letter, 1604, DD/WY/7073, DRO.
71. I ab O Edwards (ed), p65.
72. GD Owen, pp110-11.
73. I ab O Edwards (ed), p69; GD Owen, pp34-35.
74. I ab O Edwards (ed), p59.
75. I ab O Edwards (ed), p67: 'riotous assemblies ... lying in wait' were also active at this time at Eglwysbach and Glan Tal-y-cafn, p57, but these parts of old Denbighshire are now in the County Borough of Conwy.
76. *ibid*, p61.
77. *ibid*, p67.
78. *ibid*, p68.
79. *ibid*, p66.
80. *ibid*, p71.
81. *ibid*, pp166, 171.
82. *ibid*, p171.
83. *ibid*, p172.
84. *ibid*, p170.
85. *ibid*, p174.
86. *ibid*, p171.
87. TIJ Jones (ed), *Exchequer Proceedings concerning Wales in tempore James I*, p166.
88. I ab O Edwards (ed), p174.
89. *ibid*, p174.
90. *ibid*, p173.
91. *ibid*, p173.
92. *ibid*, p172.
93. *ibid*, p173.
94. *ibid*, p172.
95. *ibid*, p173.
96. *ibid*, p173. Trouble over tithes was not a fresh occurrence in the region, and there were numerous disturbances because of it during the 1880s and 1890s.
97. I ab O Edwards (ed), pp168, 170.
98. *ibid*, p167.
99. E Cane, to Sir T Hanmer, 12 Aug 1613, Bettisfield Park Collection, Record 47; Catalogue Notes, NLW.
100. Regarding the lack of public records and calendars of them, PH. Jones, *A Bibliography of the History of Wales* [Microfiche]; NLW Depts of Printed Books/Manuscripts, conversations, 1995.
101. Skeel, pp263-64.
102. See, for instance, M. Ashley, *England in the 17th. century*, pp167-213.
103. Dodd, *Studies*, p19.
104. Dodd, *Industrial*, p28.
105. On food prices and the trade cycle, Bindoff, pp198, 200; Ashley, pp24-25.
106. V Price, *The Old Meeting*, p153.
107. M Beloff, *Public order and popular disturbances, 1660-1714*, p54.
108. J Williams, Erddig, to J Edisbury, London, 29 May 1709, Erddig Manuscripts, D/E/539, FRO; also see, KL Gruffydd 'The Vale of Clwyd Corn Riots of 1740' *Flintshire Historical Society Publication* (FHS), 27 (1975-76) p36; TS Ashton/J Sykes, p116.
109. GM Griffiths, pp93-95, 108-111.
110. H Meredith, Chirk, to Rev Lloyd, 17 Feb. 1711, Chirk Manuscripts, E6120, NLW.
111. Rude, p34.
112. PDG Thomas 'Jacobitism in Wales', *Welsh History Review* (WHR), (1961) pp287-88.
113. AN Palmer *A history of the town of Wrexham* , p9.
114. On the riots of 1715-16 across the UK, see Rude, p34. In regard to these travails in Wrexham, Rev J Kenrick Diary extracts in, *Evening Leader* , 15 May 1981, NCD/459, FRO; Palmer, *Town of Wrexham* p9; *A history of the older Non-Conformity of Wrexham and its neighbourhood*, pp62-64~97; AH Dodd 'Tory Wrexham' in AH Dodd (ed) *A history of Wrexham*, pp76-77; Price, *Old*, pp153-57; HM Vaughan, 'Welsh Jacobitism'

Cymrodorion Transactions (CT) (1920-21), pp18-19; PDG Thomas, *WHR,* p288; GG Lerry, *The collieries of Denbighshire,* p15; GM Griffiths, *DHST,* p111.
115. Dodd (ed), p79.
116. H Lloyd, Ruthin, to J Myddleton, Chirk, 17 Feb. 1721, Chirk MS E5512, NLW.
117. Case Papers and Depositions re rioting in Wrexham on 5 November 1722, 6 Nov 1722, Erddig MS, D/E/2468, FRO.
118. Dodd, *ibid,* p79.
119. T Lloyd, to D. Williams, 9-11 June 1724, Chirk MS, E2070, NLW.
120. Depositions to JPs, T Eaton and R Lloyd, 10 April 1734, Glynne Papers, in Bell-Jones MSS, D/BJ/381, FRO.
121. E Thelwall, Flint, to Sir George Wynne, Leeswood, c1734, Rhual Manuscripts, D/HE/782, FRO.
122. Deposition by H Lewis, to N Griffith, JP, 6 Feb, 1735, Rhual MS, D/HE/784, FRO.
123. Depositions to N Griffith, 28 May 1737; Deposition to N Griffith and T Griffith, 30 May 1737, Rhual MS, D/HE/786, 787, FRO.
124. D Williams, to J. Myddleton, Chirk, 1 June 1740; J Griffith, to J Myddleton, 2 June 1740, Chirk MS, E4894, E87, NLW; Ashton/Sykes, pp117, 119, 121, 131; Gruffydd, pp36-40; Dodd, *ibid,* p79; Rude, p36; D Winterbottom *The Vale of Clwyd – a short history,* p52; WJ Lewis *Lead mining in Wales,* p277; GH Jenkins, *The foundations of modern Wales,* pp260, 327-29.Also, on military aid to the civil power, see TL Jones 'Military Aid to the Civil Power in Clwyd, 1715-1914', *Clwyd Historian,* Spring 1997 and B Owen, *History of the Welsh Militia and Volunteer Corps, 1757-1908, Denbighshire and Flintshire Regiments of Militia.*
125. Gruffydd, pp41-42.
126. Palmer, *Town of Wrexham,* pp297-98; Vaughan, *CT,* p23; D Nicholas, 'The Welsh Jacobites', *CT,* pp467, 471.
127. Jenkins, pp261, 327.
128. Lord Hardwicke, to Mr Warburton, 21 Aug 1753, Bettisfield MS, 80, NLW.
129. Jenkins, pp260, 327-28.
130. G. Rogers, *Brymbo and its neighbourhood,* p195; AH Dodd, 'The North Wales coal mining industry during the Industrial Revolution' *Archaeologia Cambrensis* (AC) (1929), p220; *Industrial,* p399, *Industrial,* p60; E Rogers, 'Labour struggles in Flintshire, 1830-50, Part 1' *FHS Publication* , 14 (1953-54), p47.
131. Dodd, *Industrial,* p400; DJV Jones, *Crime in 19th century Wales* p97; *Before Rebecca – popular protests in Wales, 1793-1835* p13.
132. Ashton/Sykes, pp127-28, 130-31; W J Lewis, p277; Rude, p38; DJV Jones, 'The Corn Riots in Wales, 1793-1801', *WHR* 2 (1964) p323.
133. Home Secretary, WW Grenville, to Wrexham Magistrates, 4 Aug; to C Browne, High Sheriff of Denbighshire, 15, 22 Aug 1789, in H Bristow, Catalogue 301, (7 June 1990), NTD851, FRO; J Jones to C Browne/JPs, 6 Aug 1789, in GG Lerry, 'The Wrexham Riot of 1789' (Unpublished paper, 1969), NTD144 (a), (b), FRO; Dodd, *Industrial,* p400; (ed) p81.
134. DJV Jones, *Rebecca,* p33.
135. T Boydell, to Rev HW Eyton, Wrexham, 5, 16 Aug 1787; 7 Feb, 8,31 Aug, 9 Dec 1790; 28 May 1791, Leeswood MS, D/LE/680; Sir R Mostyn, London, to Rev HW Eyton, 4, 22 May 1793, Leeswood MS, D/LE/682, 683; J Hutchison, Pool, to Rev HW Eyton, March 1794, Leeswood MS, D/LE/687, FRO; RB Clough, to J Lloyd, 27 April 1793, MS 12417C, NLW; DJV Jones, *Rebecca,* pp40-41, 43, 45-46; DG Evans, 'The Hope Enclosure Act of 1791', *FHS Journal,* 31 (1983) pp175-81.
136. Col LES Parry/Lt BFM Freeman (eds) in *Historical Records of the Denbighshire Hussars Imperial Yeomanry, 1795-1906,* p5; Resolution of a meeting re the internal defence of Denbigh, 1794, D/GW/B/1178, FRO.
137. On the 1795 riot, T Hanmer, to J Lloyd, 7 April 1795, MS 12419D, NLW; Sir GAW Evelyn-Shuckburgh, to J Lloyd, 7 Oct 1795, MS 12418D, NLW; Sir J Banks, to J Lloyd, 20 April 1795, MS 12415C, NLW; RB ap Iorwerth, to Mr Williams, 23 March 1953, NTD136, FRO; D Jones, *WHR,* pp325, 329; *Rebecca,* pp14, 18-19, 21, 33, 51-53, 55, 57, 63; GA Williams 'Beginnings of Radicalism' in T Herbert/GE Jones (eds), *The re-making of Wales in the 18th century* pp124, 134-36; 'Locating a Welsh working class: the frontier years' in D Smith (ed), *A people and a proletariat* p 35; WL Davies, 'The riot at Denbigh in 1795 – Home Office correspondence', *The Bulletin of the Board of Celtic Studies,* (BBCS) 4, (Nov 1927) pp61-64. On John Jones' role in later riots,

DJV Jones *Rebecca*, p62; and on his flight from Denbighshire in 1795, and his trials in absentia during 1795 and 1800, whereby he was twice acquitted by juries, A Owen, Denbigh, to Miss Anwyl, Vachlwyd, 27 Aug 1800, Facsimile 369/12302, NLW.

138. DJV Jones, *WHR*, p329; *Rebecca*, p21; WL Davies, *ibid*, p65.

139. WL Davies, *ibid*, p64; DJV Jones *ibid*, p329; EW Williams *Abergele – the story of a parish*, pp63-64.

140. WL Davies, *ibid*, p69; EW Williams *ibid*, pp63-64; DJV Jones, *ibid*, p329.

141. Regarding fears of rioting in Denbigh and the action taken there and in other towns, WL Davies *ibid*, pp70, 72; DJV Jones, *Rebecca*, p22; *WHR*, p331; Lt BFM Freeman 'The Flintshire Yeomanry Cavalry, 1797-1838' (Appendix 1) in Col LES Parry/Lt BFM Freeman (eds) pi. For details of the Holywell workhouse scheme and the Holywell Vestry's action refer to TL Jones *The Holywell Workhouses*, p7.

142. RB ab Iorwerth, to Mr Williams, 23 March 1953, NTD136, FRO.

143. JA Thorburn, *Talargoch mine*, p46; DJV Jones, *Rebecca*, p22; *WHR*, p331; Dodd, *Industrial*, p400.

144. Dodd, *ibid*, p400; DJV Jones, *Rebecca*, p53.

145. Sir R Mostyn, letter, 10 Feb. 1796, Leeswood MS, D/LE/736, FRO; D Jones, *Rebecca*, p168.

146. DJV Jones, *WHR*, p345.

147. DJV Jones *Rebecca* pS3.

148. Sir R Mostyn, to Rev HW Eyton, 7 Nov 1799, 21 Dec 1800, Leeswood MS, D/LE/1309, 1317, FRO.

149. On the riots of 1801, DJV Jones, *Rebecca*, pp23, 25; *WHR*, pp333-34, 336-38, 342-43; Crime in 19th century Wales, p78. On living conditions in Holywell in 1801 see, TL Jones *Living conditions in 19th century Holywell*, pp1-2.

150. On the impact of Methodism, TL Jones, *ibid*, p2. Regarding the enclosure riot, EW Williams, p63. On incendiary attacks, Dodd, *Industrial*, pp398, 401. An example of the use of this tactic in conjunction with riots as part of an overall strategy is the burning of the church at Llandrillo-yn-Rhos during the Tithe War of 1886-91. Incendiaries have been used more recently in Clwyd too, during the Meibion Glyn Dwr campaign of 1979-92.

151. DJV Jones, *Rebecca*, pp57-58, 172-73.

152. DJV. Jones, *ibid*, pp58, 69; Dodd (ed), p88; Parry/Freeman (eds), p45; G Rogers, p196.

153. E Rogers 'Labour Struggles Pt. 1' , p47; E Rogers/ (ed), R.O. Roberts 'The history of Trade Unionism in the North Wales coal mines, Part 1', p134;*Byegones* (1905-06), p41; Dodd, *Industrial*, p400; *AC*, p.220; Freeman Appendix 1 in Parry/Freeman (eds), piv; DJV Jones, *Rebecca*, p82.

154. On the situation at the time, Lerry, *Collieries*, p30. Regarding Holywell itself, Dodd, *Industrial*, p401.

155. Sir R Mostyn, to Rev HW Eyton, 12 April 1822, Leeswood MS, D/LE/1669, FRO.

156. Dodd, *Industrial*, p401; B Ellis, 'The Halkyn riots, 1866' *Llafur 5/3* , pl4.

157. WJ Lewis, p278; *Byegones* (1905-06), p41; E Rogers, 'Labour struggles Part 1', p47; Dodd, *Industrial*, p400; *AC*, p220; DJV Jones, *Rebecca*, pl92; Parry/Freeman in (eds) pp46-47; Freeman Appendix 1 in Parry/Freeman (eds), pvi; Lt BFM Freeman, 'The Royal Maylor Yeomanry Cavalry, 1803-37' Appendix 2 in Parry/Freeman (eds), pxix; B Owen 'The Yeomanry Cavalry in Flintshire, 1797-1838', pp131, 133, 136; *The Mold Riots*, p1.

158. Borough of Denbigh report to the Denbighshire Treasurer, Aug 1826; Depositions of M Jones, J Woods, to the High Constable of Denbighshire, T Jones, 8 July 1826, BD/A/189, DRO.

159. On demonstrations, DJV Jones, *Rebecca*, pl92. On the farm fires, Dodd, *Industrial*, p403.

160. For details of the socio-political malaise, including disputes about tithes, rents and wages, poverty, and demands for agricultural and political reform, see Rude, pl50. On Wales, DW Howell *Land and people in the 19th. century*, pl07.

161. On Captain Swing, EJ Hobsbawm/G Rude *Captain Swing, passim*; Rude, pp151-52, 154-55. On the Flintshire activists, Dodd, *Industrial*, p403; Freeman 'Appendix 1' in Parry/ Freeman (eds), pvi; DL Davies, 'Sir William Lloyd of Bryn Estyn in Denbighshire, Part 2' *DHST*, pp24, 27; *Byegones* (1903-04), p329; DJV Jones, *Rebecca*, p59, *Crime*, p98.

162. On the Christmas riots of 1830-31, and those of January 1831, see I Edwards 'The Wrexham Riots, Parts 1-4' *Wrexham Leader* June-July 1963, DD/ DM/228/94, FRO; D Williams 'A history of modern Wales', pp223, 235-36; AH Dodd, *A life in Wales*, pp138-39; *Industrial*, pp404-07; *AC* pp221-23; DJV Jones, *Rebecca*, pp118, 163, 175, 180, 183; Lerry, *Collieries*, pp30-33; Parry/Freeman in (eds), pp67-72, 74-77; DL Davies, *BBCS*, pp23-24; J Leach, *Coalmining – a local study,* pp45-46, 50; E Rogers, (ed), RO Roberts, 'Trade Unionism, Part

1' *FHS Journal*, 12 (1963), pp48-56; 'Trade Unionism, Part 3' *FHS Journal* 14 (1965), pp222-230, 232-35, 237-38; S Roberts 'The North Wales Coalfield strike, 1830-31, and the Wrexham riots: the development of a working class consciousness' *The Apprentice Historian* 2 (1992), pp15-17; *The Mold Riots*, p1.

163. Dodd, *Industrial*, p407; DJV Jones, *Rebecca*, pp119, 187; E Rogers 'Labour Struggles Part 1' *FHS Publication* 14, pp57-58; E Rogers (ed) RO Roberts 'Trade Unionism Part 4' *FHS Journal* 14 (1965), p229; M Bevan-Evans, 'The Mold Riot of 1831- A note' *FHS Publication* 13 (1952-53), pp72-76.

164. Parry/Freeman in (eds), p79; Freeman Appendix 1 in Parry/Freeman (eds), pviii; Major the Earl Grosvenor *Memoir of the Flintshire Yeomanry Cavalry*, pp14, 46; Dodd *ibid, pp407-08*; *AC*, p223, DJV Jones, *Ibid*, pp119-20; E Rogers 'Labour Struggles Part 1', *ibid*, pp57-59; G Rogers, p198; *Byegones*, (1903-04), p330.

165. On Chartist aims, for example, Rude, pp181-82.

166. Dodd, *Industrial*, p408; D Williams 'Chartism in Wales' in A Briggs (ed), *Chartist Studies*, p228.

167. On Chartism in Clwyd, D Egan 'Case Study 4: The Tithe War in North east Wales' in *People, protest and politics*, p98; Parry/Freeman in (eds), p89; DJV Jones *Chartism and the Chartists*, p184. Re the effects of Methodism, JT Ward *Chartism*, p246. For the Wrexham workhouse riot, GG Lerry 'The policemen of Denbighshire' *DHST* 2 (1952-53), p121.

168. Lerry, *ibid*, p109; *Collieries*, p15.

169. E Rogers/ (ed) RO Roberts 'Trade Unionism, Part 5' *FHS Journal* 15 (1966), pp146-47.

170. On Rebeccaism, for example, Rude, pp156-57.

171. Re incendiaries, DJV Jones 'Crime, protest and community in 19th century Wales' *Llafur* , 1/3 (May 1974), p10. For details of the toll gate incident at Maerdy, HT Evans, *Rebecca and her daughters*, p215. On Rebecca in Meliden, KL Morris *Talargoch lead-mine and the Meliden community, 1840-84*, p19; DJV Jones, *Crime*, p93.

172. E Rogers, 'Labour struggles in Flintshire, 1830-50, Part 2' *FHS Publication* 15 (1954-55), p105.

173. Denbighshire Spring Assizes, 1850: Brief for the Defendants and Indictment Statements, March 1850; Proofs for the Prosecution and the Defence, March 1850; Depositions, 4 March; Examination of Witnesses, 5 March 1850; Magistrates' Notice, 1 April 1850, DD/HB/361, DRO.

174. WJ Lewis, p278.

175. A Burge, 'The Mold Riots of 1869' *Llafur*, 3/3 (1982) p44.

176. KL Morris, p19.

177. RM Morris, 'The Tithe War' *DHST* 32 (1983), pp73-74.

178. E Rogers/(ed) RO Roberts, 'Trade Unionism Part 6' *FHS Journal* 16 (1967), pp113-14, 126; G Rogers p199.

179. WH Jones, 'A strike at Talargoch lead mine 100 years ago' *FHS Publication* 16 (1956), pp24-27; Thorburn, pp46, 48; DJV Jones, *Crime*, p100; KL Morris, pp25-26; Lewis, pp278-79.

180. E Rogers (ed) RO Roberts, *ibid*, pp118, 122.

181. Burge, pp43-44; CRO, *The Mold Riots*, p1; T Jones, *Leeswood and District 65 Years or so ago*, pp7-8.

182. Burge, p44.

183. DJV Jones, *Crime, protest, community and the police in 19th century Britain*, pp203, 234; *Crime*, p94. Vagrants also lit fires during a disturbance at the Holywell Union workhouse in the summer of 1867, TL Jones, *Workhouses*, p25.

184. Ellis, pp14-17; DR Hughes 'Rioting at the Halkyn mines near Holywell', *Clwyd Historian* 13 (Winter 1983-84), *passim.*

185. J Morgan, 'Denbighshire's Annus Mirabilis – the Borough and County elections of 1868', *WHR* 7 (1974), pp60-70; Burge, p44.

186. On the Leeswood and Mold riots of 1869, Day-book of PC Thomas Jones, (Leeswood), 17 Feb 1868-26 Dec 1869, FP/3/S, FRO; Public Record Office Papers relating to the Mold Riots, 1869: Chief Constable of Flintshire, P Browne, Deposition, 1869; Witnesses' Depositions, 1869, (Documents 2349); Report to the Lord-Lieutenant of Flintshire by the Clerks to the Justices, 4 June; Clerks to the Justices, to Home Office, 6 June; *Chester Chronicle*, 5 June 1869, (Documents 2348), FRO; JD Griffiths, 'The Mold Riots', *Deeside Advertiser*, 29 Oct. 1968, D/DM/720/11, FRO; 'The day that Mold, Flintshire, was torn by riots', *Flintshire Leader*, 7 June 1969, NC/61, FRO; Newspaper file and scrapbook on the Mold Riots; *Illustrated London News*, June 1869, D/DM/242/1; 'The Mold tragedy', *Wrexham Advertiser*, June 1869, D/DM/242/2; CRO, *The Mold Riots*, pp1-9; E Rogers (ed) JRO Roberts 'Trade Unionism Part 8', *FHS Journal*, 18 (1969), pp125-28; Burge, pp46-47, 49-50; T Jones, *Leeswood*, pp9-11; Leach, p56; DJV Jones, *Crime*, p100; HJ Tweddell, *Handy guide to Mold and* *the neighbourhood,* pp20-22.

187. Regarding Wrexham town, *The Wrexham Leader,* 14 Sept. 1979, NCD300, FRO. On the Brymbo riots, E Rogers (ed) RO Roberts, 'Trade Unionism Part 9', *FHS Journal,* 19 (1970), pp215-16.

188. Letter re the Rhos colliery riot of 1878, D/E/2803, FRO; *The Wrexham Leader, ibid.*

189. On the ructions at Ruabon, E Roger (ed) R.O. Roberts 'Trade Unionism Part 10', *FHS Journal,* 20 (1971), p193; DJV Jones, *Crime,* p100. Concerning the use of cutlasses Denbighshire Police General Order Book, 1878-1922, entry 24 April 1882, 'Cutlasses', DPD/2/1, DRO; Col Cobbe, to Maj Leadbetter, 29 April 1882, DPD/2/6, DRO. For details of the riots in the Brymbo area, *The Wrexham Leader,* 10 April 1981, NCD455, DRO; Lerry, *DHST,* p121. On Coedpoeth, E Rogers (ed) RO Rogers, *ibid,* p196; R Edwards, *Coedpoeth, past,* p24.

190. JE Messham, 'Conflict at Buckley Collieries: The Strike at the Elm and Maes-y-grug', *FHS Journal,* 33 (1992), pp151, 159-60, 168, 172-73, 183, 185-86.

191. Chief Constable's Orders, Denbighshire Police General Order Book, 13 Nov 1885, DPD/2/1, DRO. Regarding the Brymbo riot, Sir Watkin Williams Wynn, Notice to the Electors of East Denbighshire, Dec 1885, D/E/3148, FRO; *Evening Leader,* 16 Sept 1975, NCD79, DRO.

192. G Rogers, pp203-04.

193. Other historians note the similarities between the Rebecca and Tithe rioters, for example, DJV Jones, *Crime,* pp9, 92; Egan, p105.

194. The causes of the Tithe War are elaborated in *Report of an enquiry as to the disturbances connected with the levying of the tithe rent-charge in Wales,* Introduction pp3-4 [House of Commons Parliamentary Papers 1887, Vol. 38], NLW; Egan, pp93, 97-101, 104-06; DC Richter 'The Welsh Police, the Home Office, and the Welsh Tithe War of 1886-91' *WHR,* 12/1 (June 1984), pp50-55; RM Morris, *DHST,* pp51, 56 66; *The Tithe War,* pp5-6, 8, 12-14; ER Edwards *The Tithe Wars of North-East Wales,* pp4-8, 10; CRO, *The Tithe War,* pp1-2, and on its scope, p12.

195. CRO, *The Tithe War,* p2; Egan, pp106-07; Richter, p57; ER Edwards, p111; RM Morris, *DHST,* pp66-67.

196. *Report,* Introduction p4/pp.31, 146; CRO, *The Tithe War,* p2; Egan, pp107-08; Edwards, pp11-13; RM Morris, *DHST,* pp67, 69-70; *The Tithe War,* p18; KL Morris, p19; Howell, pp84-85; Richter, p58; D Williams, p263.

197. *Report,* Introduction, pp4, 9, NLW; ER Edwards, p14; Egan, p106; RM Morris, *DHST,* pp 1-72, 74; *The Tithe War,* pp19-20; Richter, p56; DJV Jones, *Crime,* p 102.

198. *Daily Post,* 12 Dec; *Flintshire Observer,* 16 Dec 1886, DD/DM/845/1, DRO; JH Lewis, Mostyn, to AJ Davies, Liverpool, 15 Dec 1886, D/L/54, FRO; North Wales newspaper, 18 June 1927, DD/DMY673/9, DRO; *Report,* Introduction, pp4-5, pp15-16, 31, 40, 96-97, 145, NLW; CRO, *The Tithe War,* pp2-3.

199. *Report,* Introduction, pp5, 31; ER Edwards, p15; RM Morris, *The Tithe War,* p20.

200. N Tucker, *Colwyn Bay – its origins and growth,* p176; Richter, p59.

201. North Wales newspaper, 18 June 1927, *ibid;* JE Vincent, *Letters from Wales,* pp30, 103; Richter, p60. The CRO's booklet, p3, and Egan, p108, mistakenly say that the Llangwm riots were in Sept 1887.

202. *Report,* Introduction, p5, p17; Transcript of Statements at the Ruthin Assizes, 1887: T Thomas, A Roberts, J Jones, DD/DM/673/4, DRO; Trial notes, 1887, DD/DM/673/5, DRO; North Wales newspaper, 2 June 1927 *ibid; Denbighshire Free Press,* 9 July; *Liverpool Courier,* 28 July 1887, DD/DM/845/1, DRO; H Gee, Denbigh, to TE Ellis, MP, 8, 16 July 1887, TE Ellis Papers, 662-3, NLW; RM Morris, *DHST,* pp74-75, 90-92; *The Tithe War,* pp21-22; Egan, pp108-09.

203. *Report,* Introduction, p.5, pp18, 32, 81; Col Cobbe, to Chief Con Leadbetter, 1 Feb 1887, DPD/2/12, DRO; *Liverpool Courier,* 28 July 1887, DD/DM/845/1, DRO; North Wales newspaper, 2 June 1927, *ibid;* Egan, pp109-110; RM Morris, *DHST,* p78; ER Edwards, pp.18, 24.

204. North Wales newspaper, 18 June 1927, *ibid.*

205. *Report,* Introduction, p5, 18; ER Edwards p18; RM Morris, *The Tithe War,* p24.

206. *Report,* Introduction, pp6-7, pp3-4, 8, 14, 19-20, 23-28, 30, 32-33, 36, 38, 40, 43, 44, 59-60, 62, 70-71; North Wales newspaper, *ibid; Evening Express,* 13 June; *Daily News,* 17 June; *Liverpool Courier,* 17 July 1887, DD/DM/845/1, DRO; Egan, p108; Richter, pp60-63; ER Edwards, pp18-20; RM Morris, *DHST,* pp74, 79, 92-94; *The Tithe War,* p25; Tucker, pp176-79.

207. CRO, *The Tithe War,* p5.

208. *North Wales Guardian,* 31 Dec 1887, 14 Jan 1888, DD/DM/845/1, DRO; J Trematick, *A historical guide to Caergwrle.*

209. *North Wales Guardian*, 14 Jan 1888, *ibid*; Richter, p74; Dunbabin, p220.

210. Affidavits re disturbance at Llanferres, Rev HW Jones, Llanferres. 1890, D/DM/764/185, FRO; AG Edwards, *Memories*, p130.

211. Denbighshire Constabulary General Order Book, 1878-1922, Entries 19 April; May 1888, D/2/1, DRO.

212. Details of Denbighshire disturbances in, Chief Constable's report on Tithe Proceedings in the County of Denbighshire, Maj Leadbetter, March June 1888, NTD/760, DRO; Sgt J Bagshaw Copy Out-Letter Book, Llangollen/Abergele, 1896-1908, newspaper cuttings, *passim*, DD/DM/418, DRO; *North Wales Guardian*, 2 June 1888; North Wales newspaper, 6 Aug 1927, DD/DM/845/1, DRO; *Denbighshire Free Press* 19 May 1888, in RM Morris, *DHST*, p95-97; *The Tithe War*, pp27-28; Egan, p109; Richter, pp64-65; Lerry, *DHST*, pp.131-33; ER Edwards, pp21-22; CRO, *The Tithe War*, p7. For Chief Con Leadbetter's new instructions, Denbighshire Constabulary General Order Book, *ibid*, Entry May 1888, 'Riots or Disturbances', DPD/2/1, DRO.

213. *Denbighshire County Herald*, 1 June 1888, DD/DM/845/1, DRO; North Wales newspaper, 6 Aug 1927, DD/DM/673/9, DRO; Notes by WC Wynne-Woodhouse, 28 Jan 1977, NTD/154, DRO.

214. On Caerwys, Affidavits of Disturbances at Caerwys, H Truby, Rhyl, 6 Nov 1890, D/DM/764/185, FRO. Re the clergy, AG Edwards, pp27, 131.

215. *Denbighshire County Herald*, 28 Dec 1888, DD/DM/845/1, DRO.

216. AG Edwards, p133; Richter, pp56-66.

217. On Llanferres, Affidavits of Disturbances at Llanferres, JE Edwards, Llanferres, Rev HW Jones, Llanferres, 1889; on Llanfihangel Glyn Myfyr, Mrs JM Davies, Llanfihangel Glyn Myfyr, 1889, D/DM/764/185, FRO.

218. Concerning Llanferres, Affidavits of Disturbances at Llanferres, Rev HW Jones, Llanferres, 1890; on Derwen, Rev JT Pritchard, Llanelidan, Rev M Hughes, Derwen, 1890, *ibid*.

219. *Liverpool Courier*, 19 June; *Wrexham Advertiser*, 21 June; *Denbighshire County Herald*, 27 June 1890, DD/DM/845/1, DRO.

220. *Liverpool Mercury*, 12 Aug; *North Wales Chronicle*, 16 Aug 1890, *ibid*.

221. *Wrexham Advertiser*, 23 Aug; *North Wales Guardian*, 23 Aug; *Denbighshire Free Press*, 23 Aug; *The Times*, 30 Aug 1890, *ibid*.

222. Chief Con Leadbetter, Report of a Quarterly Meeting on Tithe Disturbances, 16 Jan 1891, NTD/760, DRO.

223. Richter, pp66, 68; Egan, pp111-12; AG Edwards, pp133, 138, 141; RM Morris, *DHST*, pp85-87; CRO, *The Tithe War*, pp9, 11-12.

224. On the colliers' riots, G Rogers, p204; Lerry, *DHST*, pp134, 138, 147-48. For details of the activities in Buckley, T Jones, *Leeswood*, p19. On the quarrymen, DJV Jones, *Crime*, pp2, 56, 100.

225. JE Messham, 'Conflict on Buckley Common', *FHS Journal* 32 (1989), pp25, 27-29, 32-35, 44-46, 48, 53.

226. Depositions to Mold Crown Court, 12 April 1910, Insp J Williams, Flint police, Insp R Roberts, PC W Brown, PC A Waddicor, Lancashire police, FP/5/84, FRO.

227. Chief Constable JI Davies report, to Joint Standing Committee, Flintshire, 9 Feb 1911, FP/5/12, FRO.

228. Supt., Mold, to Chief Con JI Davies, 7 Aug. 1911; Chief Constable's report, to Summers & Sons, Shotton, 11 July 1911, *ibid*.

229. Lerry, *Collieries*, p52; *DHST*, p148; Chief Constable, Caernarfonshire, AA Ruck, to Chief Constable, Denbighshire, E Jones, 29 March 1912; DPD/2/43, DRO.

230. On the military riots of 1919, see Putkowski, *passim*, and on other civil dissension, for instance, Lerry, *Collieries*, p45, on colliers' riots at Wrexham and Brymbo before 1945.

231. Supt R Davies, Circular, to Chief Con JI Davies, 7 Sept; Dep Chief Con, Rhyl, 16 Sept. 1914; Williams & Williams, to HA Tilby, Clerk of the Peace, Mold, 25 Nov; Supt B Davies, to I Davies, 23 May 1915; Court Papers, July 1917, FC/C/6/6, FRO; JW Jones, *Rhyl, the town and its people*, p92; CJ Williams 'An anti-German riot in Rhyl, 1915' *FHS Publication* 26 (1973-74), pp171-72.

Bibliography

1. Primary unpublished sources:

Flintshire Record Office, Hawarden, Flintshire.
Disturbances caused by corn speculators at Wrexham, 1709 D/E/539.
Papers re rioting when dancing masters and players were banned from the Town Hall, and when objections were raised by Jacobites on 5 Nov 1722 D/E/2468.
Depositions re election riot at Caergwrle, 10 April 1734 D/BJ/381.
Notes on Caergwrle, 1734 NT/144.
Election riots at Flint 1734, 1737:
   Rhual Manuscripts:
      E Thelwall, Flint, to Sir G Glynne Leeswood, on legal proceedings against W Pritchard *et al*, 1734 D/HE/782.
      Deposition by H Lewis, Flint, re death of J Roberts, Flint, 1734. D/HE/784.
      Depositions by M Jones, C.Fiennes, M Evans J Cross, R Rogers, J Williams, M Rogers, R Jones, Flint, 1737 D/HE/786.
      Depositions by O Lewis, Wepra, R Abel, Flint, re affray at Flint following election of Sir G Wynne, 4 May 1737 D/HE/787.
      London Gazette article on the Jacobite Rebellion of 1745 D/M/7205.
      Resolution of a meeting re the internal defence of Denbigh, 1794. D/GW/B/1178.

   Leeswood manuscripts:
      Correspondence re enclosure riots in Flintshire, 1793-94 D/LE/682, 683, 687.
      Letter re grain riots in Mold and Rhuddlan, 1796 D/LE/736.
      Letter re corn shortage in Flintshire, 1796 D/LE/1309, 1317.
      Letters re enclosure riots, 1790 D/LE/677, 680.
      Letter re the Flintshire Yeomanry Cavalry, D/LE/1659.
      Opinions on how to deal with the Flintshire grain shortage, 1822 D/LE/1669.

Note on Mold Riot, 1831 D/HA/1275.
Notes on the Flintshire and Denbighshire Yeomanry. NT/1103.
Pamphlet on the Flintshire and Denbighshire Yeomanry. D/DM/340/22.
Rolls and Reports of the Flintshire Yeomanry. D/HA/1261-305.
Notes on the Flintshire Yeomanry. NT/1567.

Public Record Office documents:
Files on the Mold Riots, 1869 D/CL/113.

Illustrations of the Mold Riots, 1869 D/DM/122/10, D/DM/978, 3.
Newspaper cuttings on the Mold Riots, 1869 D/DM/242/1, 2, D/DM/720/11, NC/61.
Paper on the use of troops for quelling a riot by Rhos colliers, 1878. D/E/2803.
Sir Watkin Williams Wynn, Address to the Electors of East Denbighshire, 1885 D/E/3148.
Letter re tithe agitation, 1886 D/L/54.
Affidavits of disturbances at Caerwys, Derwen, Llanarmon-yn-Ial and Llanfihangel Glyn Myfyr, 1889-90 D/DM/764/185.

Flintshire Constabulary Records:
Records list, FP/1-6.

Day-book of PC T Jones, Leeswood, 17 Feb 1868-26 Dec 1869 FP/3/5.
Letters and Report of the Chief Constable re the Hawarden Bridge labour dispute, Feb–Aug 1911 FP/5/12.
Miscellaneous Papers, including the Mold Riots, 1869 FP/5/29.
Photograph – Shotton, 1910 FP/5/30.
Depositions re unlawful assembly at Hawarden Bridge Iron Works, 12 April 1910, FP/5/84.
Correspondence re riot damage to German barber's shop, Rhyl, 1914-17, FC/C/6/6.

Denbighshire Record Office, Ruthin, Denbighshire.

Index to Borough Records, 1597-1973 BD/A.
Letter on riot in Ruthin, 1604 DD/WY/7073.
Minutes of meeting of magistrates, Denbigh, 21 May 1888 in Denbigh Quarter Sessions, QSD/CX/10.
Newspaper cutting on the Church and King Riots, 1715 NCD/459.
Notes by GG Lerry on the Wrexham riots of 1789 NTD/144(a), (b).
Sale of letters of Prime Minster WW Grenville to Wrexham Magistrates and the Sheriff of Denbighshire re the colliers' riot in Wrexham, 1789 NTD/851.
Notes on the Abergele riot, 1795 NTD/136.
Papers on the Denbigh riot, 1826 BD/A/189.
Newspaper cuttings of the Wrexham riots, 1830-31. DD/DM/228/94, DD/DM/902/22.
Paper on the riot at-Coed-y-brain, Ffrwd, 1850 DD/HB/361.
Article on lawlessness in Wrexham in the 1870s, NCD/300.
Newspaper cuttings re riot over wages at Moss colliery, 1882 NCD/455.
Newspaper cutting re the election riot at Brymbo, 1885 NCD/79.
Photo of troops and police at Llanfair Talhaern 1888, and scrapbook of newspaper cuttings, 1886-91 DD/DM/845/1.
Out-letter book, Sgt J Bagshaw, Llangollen, 1896-1908 DD/DM/418.
Tithe War Notes, 1880s NTD/760.
Correspondence re the Tithe War, 1886-1939 DD/DM/673, Parts 4, 5, 9, 12, 16, 18, 20.
Notes on the Tithe War NTD/154.
Newspaper cutting re the Tithe War at Corwen DD/DM/418/1.

Denbighshire Constabulary Records:
Record list, 1849-71 DPD.
Chief Constable's General Order Book, 1878-1922, 1878-1927. DPD/2/1, DPD/2/2.
Letter from Col Cobbe re colliers and the use of cutlasses, 29 April 1882 DPD/2/6.
Letter from the Town Clerk re a disturbance, 23 June 1886 DPD/2/11.
Letter from Col Cobbe on the police reserve and the use of the military, Feb 1887 DPD/2/12. Chief Constable's General Orders, 1881-1918 DPD/2/31.
Letter re aid from Caernarfonshire during the colliers' strike, March 1912. D/2/43.
Photographs of the 10th Hussars during the Tithe War, 1890, and album of other photographs DPD/5/22.

National Library of Wales, Aberystwyth, Ceredigion.

RB Clough, to J Lloyd, 27 April 1793 MS 12417C.
T Hanmer, to J Lloyd, 7 April 1795 MS 12419D.
Sir J Banks, to J Lloyd, 20 April 1795 MS 12415C.
Sir GAW Evelyn-Shuckburgh, to J Lloyd, 7 Oct. 1795 MS 12418D.

Bettisfield Park Collection:
E Cane, to Sir T Hanmer, 12 Aug 1613 Record 47.
Lord Hardwicke, to Mr Warburton, 21 Aug. 1753 Record 80.

Chirk Collection:
   H Meredith, to Rev Lloyd, 12 Feb 1711 E6120.
   H Lloyd, to J Myddelton, 19 Feb 1721 E5512.
   T Lloyd, to D Williams, 9-11 June 1724 E2070.
   D Williams, to J Myddleton, 1 June 1740 E4894.
   J Griffith, to J Myddelton, 2 June 1740 E87.

TE Ellis Papers:
   H Gee, to TE Ellis MP, 8 July 1887 662-3.
   H Gee, to TE Ellis MP, 16 July 1887 663.

Facsimile Collection:
   A Owen, to Miss Anwyl, 27 Aug 1800 Facs 369/12302.

Wrexham Leisure, Libraries and Culture Dept, Wrexham.

   Miscellaneous Papers on Wrexham riots.
   Newspaper cuttings on the Wrexham riots, 1830-31.

2. Primary published source:
   Regulations and Instructions for the Flintshire Yeomanry Cavalry (Flintshire: 1835)
   Report of an enquiry as to disturbances connected with the levying of tithe rent charge in Wales (London: HMSO/Eyre and Spottiswoode, 1887) [Microfiche– House of Commons Parliamentary papers, 1887, Volume 38, 93.311-12].

3. Secondary unpublished sources:
   TL Jones, *The development of British counterinsurgency policies and doctrines, 1945-52*, (University of London, 1992)

4. Secondary published sources:
   a) Articles and papers—
      Anon. 'The Tithe War in Llanarmon' *Llanarmon-yn-Iâl Local History Review* 5 (Feb 1982).
      M Bevan-Evans 'The Mold Riot of 1831- a note' *Flintshire Historical Society Publication* 13 (1952-53).
      A Burge, 'The Mold Riots of 1869', *Llafur*, 3/3 (1982).
      Bye-gones Volumes 1876, 1897, 1903-04, 1905-06.
      DL Davies, 'Sir William Lloyd of Bryn Estyn in Denbighshire, Part 2', *Denbighshire Historical Society Transactions* 26 (1977).
      WL Davies 'The Riot at Denbigh in 1795– Home Office Correspondence', *The Bulletin of the Board of Celtic Studies* 4 (Nov 1927).
      AH Dodd 'The North Wales coal industry during the Industrial Revolution', *Archaeologia Cambrensis*, (1929),
      'Tory Wrexham', in AH Dodd (ed).
      D Egan, 'Case Study 4: the Tithe War in North East Wales', in Egan.
      B Ellis 'The Halkyn Riots, 1866', *Llafur*, 5/3 (1990).
      DG Evans, 'The Hope Enclosure Act of 1791', *Flintshire Historical Society Journal*, 31 (1983).
      Lt BFM Freeman 'The Flintshire Yeomanry Cavalry, 1797-1838 (Appendix 1)', in Col LES Parry/Lt BFM Freeman (eds),
      'The Royal Maylor Yeomanry Cavalry, 1803-37 (Appendix 2)', in Parry/Freeman (eds).
      'The Ancient British (or North Wales) Fencible Cavalry, 1794-1800 (Appendix 4)' in Parry/Freeman (eds).
      GM Griffiths 'Glimpses of Denbighshire in the Records of the Court of Great Sessions',

Denbighshire Historical Society Transactions, 22 (1973).

KL Gruffydd, 'The Vale of Clwyd Corn Riots of 1740', *Flintshire Historical Society Publication*, 27 (1975-76).

DR Hughes 'Rioting at the Halkyn mines, near Holywell', *Clwyd Historian*, 13 (Winter 1983/84).

GA. Hughes, 'The Flintshire and Denbighshire Yeomanry Cavalry', (Flint Public Libraries; 1967)

DJV Jones, 'Crime, protest and community in 19th century Wales', *Llafur*, 1/3 (May 1974).

'Law enforcement and popular disturbances in Wales, 1793-1835', *Journal of Modern History*, 42/2 (1970).

'The corn riots in Wales, 1793-1801', *Welsh History Review* 2 (1964).

WH Jones, 'A strike at Talargoch lead-mine 100 years ago', *Flintshire Historical Society Publication*, 16 (1956).

GG Lerry, 'The policemen of Denbighshire', *Denbighshire Historical Society Transactions*, 2 (1953).

JE Messham, 'Conflict at Buckley collieries: the strike at the Elm and Maes-y-grug', *Flintshire Historical Society Journal*, 33 (1992).

'Conflict on Buckley Common', *Flintshire Historical Society Journal*, 32 (1989).

J Morgan, 'Denbighshire's Annus Mirabilis: the Borough and County Elections of 1868', *Welsh History Review*, 7 (1974).

RM Morris, 'The Tithe War', *Denbighshire Historical Society Transactions*, 32 (1983).

P Nicholas, 'The Welsh Jacobites', *Cymrodorion Transactions*, (1948).

P O'Leary, 'Anti-Irish riots in Wales', *Llafur*, 5/4 (1991).

B Owen, *The Flintshire Yeomanry*, (Cardiff: Royal Regiment of Wales, 1993);

'The Yeomanry Cavalry in Flintshire, 1797-1838', *Military Historical Society Bulletin*, 25/100 (May 1975).

T Price, 'The case for tithes stated simply in a few plain notes', *Rhyl Journal*, (1887).

D Richter, 'The Welsh police, the Home Office, and the Welsh Tithe War of 1886-91', *Welsh History Review*, 12/1 (June 1984).

S Roberts'The North Wales coal field strike of 1830-31 and the 'Wrexham Riots': the development of a working class consciousness', *The Apprentice Historian*, 2 (1992).

E Rogers, 'Labour struggles in Flintshire, 1830-50 Part 1', *Flintshire Historical Society Publication*, 14 (1953-54).

'Labour struggles in Flintshire, 1830-50, Part 2', *Flintshire Historical Society Publication*, 15 (1954-55).

E Rogers/(ed) RO Roberts, 'The history of Trade Unionism in the North Wales coal mines', *Flintshire Historical Society Journal*, 12 (1963).

'The history of Trade Unionism in the coal-mining industry of North Wales to 1914': Parts 3-12 *Flintshire Historical Society Journal*, 13-22 (1964-73).

PDG Thomas, 'Jacobitism in Wales', *Welsh History Review*, 2 (1961).

HM Vaughan, 'Welsh Jacobitism', *Cymrodorion Transactions*, (1920-1).

D Williams, 'Chartism in Wales', in A Briggs (ed).

GA Williams, 'Beginnings of Radicalism', in T Herbert/GE Jones (ed).

'Locating a Welsh working class: the frontier years', in D Smith (ed).

CJ Williams, 'An Anti-German Riot in Rhyl, 1915', *Flintshire Historical Society Publication*, 26 (1973-74).

LJ Williams, 'The coal owners', in D Smith (ed).

b) Books

M Ashley, *England in the 17th century* (Middlesex: Penguin, 1961)

TS Ashton/J. Sykes, *The coal industry of the 18th century* (Manchester: Manchester Univ. Press, 1929)

M Beloff, *Public order and popular disturbances, 1660-1714* (London: OUP, 1938).

ST Bindoff, *Tudor England* (Middlesex: Penguin, 1950).

A Briggs (ed), *Chartist Studies* (London: MacMillan, 1962).

R Burt/P Waite/R Burnley, *The mines of Flintshire and Denbighshire* (Exeter: Univ of Exeter Press, 1992)

A Charlesworth (ed), *An atlas of rural protest* (London: Croom Helm, 1983).

Clwyd Record Office Annual Report of the County Archivist (Hawarden: Clwyd Record Office, 1980, 1986).

The Mold Riots (Hawarden: Clwyd Record Office, 1977).

The Tithe War (Hawarden: Clwyd Record Office, 1978).

J Davies, *A history of Wales* (London: Allen Lane, 1993).

RR Davies/RA Griffiths/IG Jones/KD Morgan (eds), *Welsh society and nationhood* (Cardiff: Univ of Wales Press, 1984).

T Davies, *Religion and society in 19th century Wales* (Llandybie: Chris Davies, 1988).

AH Dodd (ed), *A history of Wrexham* (Wrexham: Hughes & Son, 1957).

Life in Wales (London: B.T. Batsford, 1972).

Studies in Stuart Wales (Mold: Clwyd County Council, 1991).

The Industrial Revolution in North Wales (Cardiff: Univ of Wales Press, 1951), (Wrexham: Bridge Books, 1971 Edition, 1991).

JPD Dunbabin, *Rural discontent in 19th century Britain* (London: Faber, 1974).

AG Edwards, *Memories* (London: J. Murray, 1927).

ER Edwards, *The Tithe Wars of North-East Wales* (Ruthin: Coelion Publications, 1989)

I ab O Edwards (ed), *A catalogue of Star Chamber Proceedings relating to Wales* (Cardiff: Univ. of Wales Press, 1929).

R.Edwards (ed), *Coedpoeth as it was* (Wrexham: Star Press, 1991).

Coedpoeth- past (Wrexham: Star Press, 1925).

D Egan, *People, protest and politics* (Llandysul: Gomer, 1987).

DG Evans, *A history of Wales, 1815-1906* (Cardiff: Univ. of Wales Press, 1989).

HT Evans, *Rebecca and her daughters* (Cardiff: Educational Publishing Co, 1910).

J Finnemore, *Social life in Wales* (London: A. & C. Black, 1922).

R Flenley (ed), *A calendar of the register of the Queen's Majesty's Council in the Marches of Wales* (London: The Honourable Society of the Cymrodorion, 1916).

Flintshire Constabulary, *Flintshire Constabulary Centenary, 1856-1956* (Holywell: 1956).

D Gater, *Battles of Wales* (Llanrwst: Gwasg Garreg Gwalch, 1991).

Major the Earl Grosvenor, *Memoir of the Flintshire Yeomanry* (Chester: T Griffith, 1838).

TH Herbert/GE Jones (eds), *The remaking of Wales in the 18th century* (Cardiff: Univ. of Wales Press, 1988).

EJ Hobsbawn/G Rude, *Captain Swing* (London: Laurence & Wishart, 1969).

DW Howell, *Land and people in the 19th century* (London: Routledge & Kegan Paul).

GH Jenkins, *The foundations of modern Wales, 1642-1780* (Oxford: OUP, 1993).

GH Jenkins/JB Smith (eds), *Politics and society in Wales, 1840-1922* (Cardiff: Univ. of Wales Press, 1988).

D Jones, *Chartism and the Chartists* (London: Allen Lane, 1975).

DJV Jones, *Before Rebecca – popular protests in Wales, 1793-1835* (London: Allen Lane, 1973).

Crime in 19th century Wales (Cardiff: Univ. of Wales Press, 1992).

Crime, protest, community and the police in 19th century Britain (London: Routledge, 1982).

EG Jones (ed), *Exchequer Proceedings (Equity) concerning Wales, Henry VIII to Elizabeth I* (Cardiff: Univ. of Wales Press, 1939).

IG Jones, *Communities* (Llandysul: Gomer, 1987).

JW.Jones, *Rhyl – the town and its people* (Rhyl: The Clwyd Press, 1970).

PH Jones, *A Bibliography of the history of Wales* (Cardiff: Univ. of Wales Press, 1989).

RM Jones, *The North Wales Quarrymen* (Cardiff: Univ. of Wales Press, 1982).

T Jones, *Leeswood and district 65 years ago and previously* (1919)

TIJ Jones (ed), *Exchequer proceedings concerning Wales in tempore James I* (Cardiff: Univ. of Wales, 1955).

TL Jones, *Living conditions in 19th century Holywell* (Mold: Ruthin Voluntary Services Council, 1995).

The Holywell workhouses (Greenfield: Valuprint, 1995).

I Kelly, *The North Wales coalfield – a collection of pictures*, Volume 1 (Wrexham: Bridge Books, 1990).

J Leach, *Coalmining – a local study* (Wrexham: Wrexham Humanities Project, 1984).

GG Lerry, *The collieries of Denbighshire* (Wrexham: W Williams, 1968).

EA Lewis (ed), *An inventory of early Chancery Proceedings concerning Wales* (Cardiff: Univ. of Wales, 1937).

EA Lewis/JC Davies (eds), *Records of the Court of Argumentations relating to Wales and Monmouthshire* (Cardiff: Univ of Wales press, 1954).

WJ Lewis, *Lead-mining in Wales* (Cardiff: Univ of Wales Press, 1967).

P Morgan/D.Thomas, *Wales: the shaping of a nation* (Newton Abbot: David & Charles, 1984).

KL Morris, *Talargoch lead-mine, and the Meliden community, 1840-84* (Denbigh: Gee & Son, 1990).

RM Morris, *The Tithe War* (Oxford: OUP, 1989).

GD Owen, *Elizabethan Wales* (Cardiff: Univ of Wales Press, 1964).

AN Palmer, *A history of the older Non-Conformity of Wrexham and its neighbourhood* (Wrexham: Woodall, Minshall and Thomas, nd, c1888).

A history of the town of Wrexham (Wrexham: Woodall, Minshall and Thomas, 1893).

Col LES Parry/Lt BFM Freeman (eds), *Historical Records of the Denbighshire Hussars Imperial Yeomanry* (Wrexham: Woodall, Minshall, Thomas & Co, 1909).

V Price, *The Old Meeting* (Wrexham: E Jones, nd, c1935).

RE Prothero, *The anti-tithe agitation in Wales* (London: Guardian Office, 1889).

J Putkowski, *The Kinmel Park Riots, 1919* (Denbigh: Flintshire Historical Society, 1989).

G Roberts, *Aspects of Welsh history* (Cardiff: Univ of Wales Press, 1969).

AJ Roderick (ed), *Wales through the Ages* (Swansea: Chris Davies, 1960).

Wales through the Ages 2 (Swansea: Chris Davies, 1975).

G Rogers, *Brymbo and its neighbourhood* (Wrexham: the author, 1991).

G Rude, *The crowd in history* (London: Laurence & Wishart, 1981).

M Salmon, *A source-book of Welsh history* (London: OUP, 1927).

CAJ Skeel, *The Council of the Marches of Wales* (London: Hugh Rees Ltd, 1904).

D Smith (ed), *A people and a proletariat* (London: Pluto, 1980).

JA Thorburn, *Talargoch mine* (Sheffield: Northern Mine Research Society, 1986).

JJ Tobias, *Crime and industrial society in the 19th century* (London: BT Batsford, 1967).

J Trematick, *A historical guide to Caergwrle* (Wrexham: The Print Project, nd).

N Tucker, *Colwyn Bay – its growth and origin* (Colwyn Bay: Colwyn Bay Borough Council, 1953)

HJ Tweddell, *Handy guide to Mold and the neighbourhood* (Mold: WM Bellamy, 1890).

JE Vincent, *Letters from Wales* (London: WH Allen, 1889).

The land question in Wales (London: Longmans, Green & Co, 1896).

JT Ward, *Chartism* (London; BT Batsford, 1973).

P Warner, *Famous Welsh Battles* (London: Fontana, 1977).

D Williams, *A history of modern Wales* (London: J Murray, 1977).

The Rebecca Riots (Cardiff: Univ of Wales Press, 1955).

EW Williams, *Abergele – the story of a parish* (Denbigh: Gee & Son, 1968).

G Williams, *Religion, language and nationality in Wales* (Cardiff: Univ of Wales Press, 1979).

J Williams, *Ancient and modern Denbigh* (Mold: Clwyd County Council, 1989).

P Williams, *The Council in the Marches of Wales under Elizabeth I* (Cardiff: Univ of Wales Press, 1958).

WL Williams, *The making of modern Wales* (London: Macmillan, 1919).

D Winterbottom, *The Vale of Clwyd – a short history* (Denbigh: Gee & Son, 1982).